Are Catholics

A Guid

Evangelical Questions about the Catholic Church

by

Shane Schaetzel

Regnum Dei Press

MMXX

November 2020
Second Edition

Unless otherwise indicated, all Scripture references are taken from the Douay-Rheims 1899 American Edition

Cover Photo by Juan de Juanes
The Last Supper
AD 1562
Public Domain

To my family:
Penny, Michael & Lauren

May they never be timid
to proclaim their faith.

CONTENTS

CONTENTS 7

FOREWORD
by Father Chori Seraiah 13

INTRODUCTION 15

CHAPTER 1: GENERAL QUESTIONS 21

Are Catholics Christians? 21

Do Catholics believe in Jesus Christ? 21

What do Catholics mean by the Holy Trinity? 22

Is Catholicism a cult? 24

Do some Catholic practices have Pagan origin? 26

Must a person understand Latin to be a Catholic? 29

Is the Catholic Church opposed to modern science? 30

Why is Catholic worship so organized and structured compared to most Protestant worship? 31

Why is the Catholic Church so rich when so many of its members are poor? 33

Many Christians believe all sins are equal, do Catholics believe this too? 35

What is the Catholic Church's position on sexual sin? 36

What is the Catholic Church's position on abortion? 38

What is the Catholic Church's position on artificial contraception? 39

Are Catholics socialists? 43

Are all Catholics the same? 44

CHAPTER 2: SPECIFIC QUESTIONS 47

Why do Catholics call priests "father" when the Bible says "call no man father?" 47

Why do Catholics confess their sins to a priest when they could go directly to God? 49

Why can't Catholic priests be married? 50

Why does the Catholic Church not ordain women? 54

Why do some Catholic women wear head-coverings in church? 59

Are Catholics allowed to divorce? 61

Isn't an annulment just a Catholic divorce? 64

Why do Catholics and Protestants number the Ten Commandments differently? 65

Why do Catholics use the rosary when the Bible says not to pray in "vain repetitions?" 67

Is the pope the Antichrist? 69

Wasn't Constantine the first pope? 71

Didn't Constantine invent the Catholic Church and introduce Pagan beliefs into Christianity at that time? 74

Isn't the Catholic Church the "Whore of Babylon" from the Book of Revelation? 75

Doesn't God hate religion, and isn't Christianity really about having a personal relationship with God? 78

CHAPTER 3: THE BIBLE 81

Do Catholics believe in the Bible? 81

Do Catholics read the Bible? 82

Why do Catholic Bibles have more books than Protestant Bibles? 83

Do Catholics follow the Bible alone? 87

Wait! Doesn't the Bible tell us to follow the Bible alone? 89

Didn't the medieval Catholic Church chain Bibles to altars, burn vernacular Bible translations and intentionally try to prevent the people from reading the Scriptures by keeping them in Latin? 93

CHAPTER 4: MARY AND THE SAINTS 97

Do Catholics worship Mary? 97

If Catholics don't worship Mary, why do they pray to her? 97

Why pray to Mary and the Saints at all, when you can take your prayers directly to God? 98

How is praying to the Saints not necromancy or witchcraft which is forbidden in the Bible? 99

Why do Catholics have statues of Mary and other Saints? 101

Doesn't the Bible forbid the use of statues and "graven images?" 101

Why do Catholics believe in the ever virginity of Mary when the Bible talks about the "brothers" of Jesus Christ? 103

Why do Catholics believe Mary was without sin? 104

Do Catholics believe Mary ascended to Heaven like Jesus? 107

Why do Catholics give so much honor to Mary? 109

CHAPTER 5: SALVATION 113

Are Catholics "saved" or "born again?" 113

Do Catholics believe in salvation by faith alone? 114

Do Catholics believe in "once saved, always saved?" 116

Why do Catholics baptize babies when they can't even understand what is going on? 116

Do Catholics believe purgatory is a place between heaven and hell? 119

Do Catholics believe Evangelicals can be saved? 120

Do Catholics believe in the Rapture? 121

CHAPTER 6: THE SACRAMENT 125

Do Catholics really believe that communion bread and wine become the literal flesh and blood of Jesus Christ? 125

So does this mean that Catholics believe Jesus is re-crucified every time a priest says the Mass? 127

Do Catholics believe Protestant communion is the same as Catholic communion? 128

So then is Protestant communion just symbolic? 128

So if Catholics believe the communion elements are literally the manifestation of Jesus Christ, who is God, does that mean that Catholics worship these communion elements as God? 129

How is the Catholic worship of bread and wine not idolatry? 130

How can this Catholic worship of communion elements be Biblical? 131

How can any reasonable and sane person be expected to believe such absurdity as the transubstantiation of bread and wine into the literal flesh and blood of Jesus Christ? 132

CHAPTER 7: THE CHURCH **135**

Do Catholics really believe the Catholic Church is the one and only Church ever established by Jesus Christ? 135

So do Catholics believe Evangelical churches are illegitimate? 137

How can Catholics say that Peter is the "rock" upon which Jesus built the Church, when clearly the passage used to support this uses two completely different words for "rock?" 139

How can Peter (Cephas) be the "rock" when the Apostle Paul calls Jesus Christ the "rock?" 143

How can Catholics say Peter died in Rome, when there is no Biblical record of Peter ever being in Rome? 143

Maybe Jesus did invest his authority into his Apostles, but does that mean these Apostles could really transfer that authority on to their successors? 146

Why do we need Apostolic successors when we have the Bible? 147

How can the Catholic Church really be the Church Jesus established when there are scandals and corruption? 147

Do Catholics really believe the pope is infallible? 152

CONCLUSION **155**

APPENDIX 1: List of Pontificates **161**

APPENDIX 2: The Biblical Canon **171**

RESOURCES **175**

FOREWORD
by Father Chori Seraiah

As a convert myself, there have been many times that I encountered people telling me that I should not have become Catholic. They each have their own reasons, and many of them are quite similar. All in all, they all have one thing in common though: they all point to something that they reject which is not actually a doctrine or practice of the Catholic faith. As Archbishop Fulton Sheen said so profoundly many years ago: there are only a few people who reject the Catholic Church, but there are many who reject what they *mistakenly believe* the Catholic Church to be.

This is something that we as Catholics have to deal with. When someone says that he left the Church, or that he does not want to be Catholic, it is important for us to seek to understand why. It is becoming more and more common that those reasons why are based on faulty perspectives and misrepresentations of the Catholic Church. Shane Schaetzel has helped us to overcome this problem.

I met Shane before I was even Catholic, and now it is my joy to be his priest (God's providence is always amazing, is it not?). I am happy to say that he has done a great work to help us spread the truth about the Catholic Church and her teachings. His book, *Are Catholics Christian?*, takes its place in the work of the growth of the Kingdom of God by clarifying what the Church really does, and does not, say.

Certainly we do not want anyone to reject the Catholic faith, because we believe in doing so they are rejecting the salvation of Christ Himself. It is our responsibility, therefore, to do what we can to help people know the truth. That is the heart of evangelism. Whether used in RCIA catechism classes, or just being handed to a non-catholic by a Catholic, this book should be used for the spreading of the truth of Christ our Lord.

Fr. Chori Jonathin Seraiah
St. George Catholic Church
Republic, Missouri

INTRODUCTION

Roman Catholics, living in the Ozark Mountains, know what it's like to be a minority religion in the "Bible Belt" of the United States. Since most Christians in this part of America are ***Evangelicals***,[1] they often have little knowledge of what the Catholic Church really is, or what Catholics really believe. They may even have some misunderstandings. This book is in a Question and Answer format, designed specifically for people in this area, or anyone else who might have a similar curiosity. I will intentionally try to keep the answer to each question as brief as I possibly can for this purpose, yet still be detailed enough so as to give a respectable explanation. The following is a compilation of real questions I have actually received from real Evangelicals here in the Ozark Mountains of Southern Missouri and Northern Arkansas.

The reader may take note of my liberal usage of the word "Protestant" in this book. I am quite aware that some Evangelical Christians object to usage of this word in reference to them. I assure the reader that when I use the word "Protestant," there is no ill intent. It is simply a classification, much in the same way the word "Catholic" is a classification. There are many different kinds of Catholics.

[1] According to Merriam-Websters, Evangelical is defined as a type of Protestant "emphasizing salvation by faith in the atoning death of Jesus Christ through personal conversion, the authority of Scripture, and the importance of preaching as contrasted with ritual." This is most clearly seen in nondenominational churches and various denominations, including but not limited to: Baptist, Pentecostal, Charismatic, Methodist, etc.

There are: Roman Catholics, Byzantine Catholics, Maronite Catholics, Franciscans, Benedictines, Carmelites, Traditional Catholics and even English Patrimony Catholics. Yet they are all Catholics in union with Rome and under the authority of the pope. The same goes for Protestants. There are many different kinds: Anglican, Lutheran, Methodist, Presbyterian, Baptist, Pentecostal, Nondenominational and those who simply wish to be called "born again Christians." Yet they are all Protestants in a general sense, in that their spiritual roots can be easily traced back to the sixteenth-century Protestant Reformation. Traditionally, the word "Protestant" has been used for mainline traditional denominations (Anglican, Lutheran, Methodist, Reformed, etc.); while Christians outside these denominations have been referred to under the general term "Evangelical." For the purpose of this book, and its intended audience, I'll use the words "Protestant" and "Evangelical" interchangeably. As it is the Evangelical type of Protestant that this book will most appeal to.

The reader may also notice that the majority of the questions contained herein deal primarily with Evangelical concerns. Whereas, traditional Protestants might not have the same concerns. Here in the Bible Belt of the United States, the overwhelming vast majority of Protestants are Evangelical. Demographic analysis, over the last thirty years, shows that Evangelicals now make up the majority of Protestants, both in the United States, and around the world. They are also growing at such an exponential rate, it's only a matter of time before they completely dominate the entire Protestant ethos. At this present rate, within less than a generation, these groups will represent the overwhelming vast majority of all Protestantism. Oh sure, mainline traditional denominations are not going away anytime soon. They have enough resources to hang on for a good long time, but in comparison to Evangelical groups, their rate of growth is very modest, and in some cases, even regressive. Therefore, the majority of questions Catholics deal with in the Bible Belt, will soon be the majority of questions all Catholics will deal with wherever Protestants are numerous. Thus, the questions addressed in this book should become increasingly more relevant worldwide as time progresses.

At this point, a little background information is probably in order. I am a Roman Catholic layman[2] of the English Patrimony.[3] I'm also a catechist[4] and a fourth-degree knight,[5] but this was not always the case. I was actually baptized in the Missouri Synod of the Lutheran Church shortly after my birth in Southern California. My father was Lutheran, and comes from a long line of Lutherans stretching back to the sixteenth century in Germany. My mother was raised Southern Baptist in Western Tennessee. As a compromise, my parents raised my sisters and I in the

---

[2] Layman: one who is not ordained as a cleric. In other words, a regular church goer, and not a professional minister.

[3] English Patrimony: the liturgy, customs, traditions and music brought back into the Catholic Church from Anglicanism. Typically, the English Patrimony is found in the Personal Ordinariates of the Catholic Church, located in the United Kingdom, North America and Oceania.

[4] Catechist: meaning one who is formally trained to teach the Catholic Faith, traditionally in a question-answer format.

[5] The Knights of Columbus is a global Catholic fraternal service order. Membership is composed of practicing Catholic men.

American Baptist Church[6] which held to Baptist doctrine but was a bit more liturgical in practice, similar to Methodist in a lot of ways. Upon reaching adulthood, I branched out on my own, looking for the Church I believed to have the most continuity with early Christianity. I eventually settled on an Evangelical nondenominational church where I met Penny, the woman who would eventually become my wife. Penny was baptized Methodist, but was raised in a variety of religious traditions. Together we lived as Evangelicals while I studied for the ministry.

It was through these studies that I discovered the Jewish roots of the Christian faith and the writings of the early Church fathers. You'll notice I cite these writings throughout this book, both by quotation and footnote. This is because in order to understand what early Christians believed and practiced, we need to read what they left behind for us in their writings. The early Christians were prolific writers for their time, and they left for us a rather detailed record. From these writings, combined with the sacred Scriptures, we can reconstruct a fairly accurate image of what the early Church was like. In these writings, I found a continuity with ancient Judaism of course, but I also discovered them to be much more "catholic" than I was comfortable with. My understanding of Christian doctrine began to change with this, and in time, I could no longer preach what I truly believed on Sunday mornings when I filled in for the pastor. At this point, Penny and I quietly left our Evangelical church and began looking for a place where

[6] American Baptist Church (ABC), informally called "Northern Baptists"

we could familiarize ourselves with catholic traditions in what we believed to be a "good, safe, Protestant environment." We eventually settled down as Anglicans in a moderately conservative Episcopal Church.

We loved this little Episcopal Church, we loved its priest, and we particularly loved the liturgy of the Anglican tradition. It seemed to solve a great deal of problems for us, and we would have stayed there were it not for the overtly progressive direction of the national denomination. We looked into more conservative Anglican alternatives, but at that time, our area didn't have any of reasonable size. Penny felt uncomfortable moving to a smaller church and wanted something larger if we were no longer going to stay with the Episcopal Church. It was at this point I knew we had to make a choice between Roman Catholicism or Eastern Orthodoxy.

So I seriously began looking into the doctrines of both institutions and, for the first time in my life, compared them with the teachings of early Christianity. Both Catholicism and Orthodoxy were very appealing for similar reasons, but in the end, it all came down to the issue of Christian authority. We chose the Roman Catholic Church and received the sacraments of Confirmation and Holy Eucharist at Saint Elizabeth Ann Seton Church in Springfield, Missouri, on the 22nd day of April, in the year of our Lord 2000. It was the Easter Vigil. Since then we have been blessed with two children and both were baptized in the Catholic Church.

I have dedicated this book to my family, who I hope will never take their Catholic Christian faith for granted, nor be embarrassed to call themselves Catholic. For sometimes, when other Christians are quick to judge or discriminate because of our Catholicism, it's easy to give up and try to blend in. May this never be the case. We Catholics are very Biblical Christians, more so than most Evangelicals know, and I hope this book will effectively demonstrate that.

CHAPTER 1: GENERAL QUESTIONS

Are Catholics Christians?

Yes, Catholics are not only Christians, but we were the first Christians. The Roman Catholic Church is the oldest Christian Church founded by Jesus Christ in AD 33, and planted in Rome in about AD 42,[7] when Saint Peter established his Apostolic see in Rome after planting a church in Antioch.[8] Peter was later crucified in Rome, upside down, in the year AD 67.[9] His direct successors became the popes.

Do Catholics believe in Jesus Christ?

Yes, of course we believe in Jesus Christ. We believe he is God the Son – the Second Person of the Holy Trinity (Father, Son and Holy Spirit) – made flesh and blood, taking on a fully human form, and becoming fully man in every way, yet retaining his full divinity.[10] We believe in his life, virgin birth, miracles, ministry, suffering, death and resurrection. We also believe he is currently reigning as the

---

[7] Irenaeus, Against Heresies, 3:1:1 (AD 180); Eusebius of Caesarea, The Chronicle (AD 303)

[8] Clement of Rome, The First Epistle of Clement, 5 (AD 96); Irenaeus, Against Heresies, 3:1:1 (AD 180); Eusebius, Church History, 2:14,5 (AD 325)

[9] Gauss, fragment in Eusebius' Church History, 2:25 (AD 198); Tertian, Against Marcion, 4:5 (AD 210); Tertullian, Scorpiace,15:3 (AD 212); Peter of Alexandria, The Canonical Epistle, Canon 9 (AD 306); Cyril of Jerusalem, Catechetical Lectures, 6:14-15 (AD 350)

[10] Catechism of the Catholic Church, paragraphs 464 - 470, 480 - 482

King of kings in Heaven, and he will one day return to judge the living and the dead.[11]

What do Catholics mean by the Holy Trinity?

We believe in ONE God, who is eternally existent in three divine Persons: Father, Son and Holy Spirit.[12] This is the teaching of the Holy Scriptures[13] and the early Church. The first Christians gave their lives for this faith. As Justin Martyr wrote in AD 155: *"Our teacher of these things is Jesus Christ, who also was born for this purpose, and was crucified under Pontius Pilate, procurator of Judaea, in the times of Tiberius Caesar; and that we reasonably worship Him, having learned that He is the Son of the true God Himself, and holding Him in the second place, and the prophetic Spirit in the third, we will prove."* – (Justin Martyr, First Apology 13)

The doctrine of the Trinity was taught from the earliest days of the Church, and it's helpful to remember that the people who gave their lives as martyrs in the Roman circuses (made into human torches and lion food) died believing that Jesus Christ is God, and that he is the second Person of the Holy Trinity. The name "Trinity" was used as early as the third century to briefly describe the triune nature of God. The doctrine was finally defined dogmatically in the early fourth century at the Council of Nicea in response to

[11] Catechism of the Catholic Church; pages 56 - 57

[12] Catechism of the Catholic Church, paragraphs 232, 234, 237, 261 & 266

[13] Matthew 3:16-17; Matthew 28:19; John 1:1; John 8:59-59; John 10:30-33; John 14:26; John 15:26; John 20:28; 2nd Corinthians 13:14; Galatians 4:4-6; Titus 2:13

the Arian heresy.[14] Thus, the Catholic Christian faith was dogmatically defined as those Christians who maintained belief in the Trinity, as opposed to those who followed Arius in denying the Trinity.

The doctrine of the Trinity is universally accepted by all Christian churches that broke with the Catholic Church in the sixteenth century and thereafter. It is taught by all Christian churches connected to the Catholic Church through history and baptism. It is the universal doctrine of all Protestant denominations: Lutheran, Anglican, Methodist, Reformed, Presbyterian, Baptist, Pentecostal, etc. Evangelicals are staunchly Trinitrian in their belief about God. Christianity has always been defined as a Trinitarian faith, meaning the belief in ONE God in three equally divine Persons. There are of course some churches that no longer teach the Trinity. These churches are no longer connected to the Catholic Church, neither through history nor baptism. For that matter, they are no longer connected to Protestantism or Evangelicalism, and most of them have no problem telling you that.

[14] Arian heresy: In the early fourth century, a rogue priest named Arius introduced the teaching that Jesus Christ is not divine and that God is not a Trinity. This caused such a great disturbance in the early Church that an ecumenical council was called in the City of Nicea (located in Asia Minor) in which all of the bishops were summoned to investigate this matter. They condemned the Arian heresy, affirmed the Trinity as the universal faith taught by the Apostles, formulated the Nicene Creed, and ordered the compilation of a universal New Testament to combat this heresy.

Is Catholicism a cult?

This is a fun question. When some Protestants call Catholicism a "cult," there has never been a better example of the proverbial *pot calling the kettle "black!"* Religions are defined by their definition of God. If Catholicism is a "cult," then so is every Protestant denomination and affiliation, as they all subscribe to the same Catholic doctrine of the Holy Trinity and belief that Jesus Christ is God.

Protestants (particularly Evangelicals) are connected to Catholicism both through history and baptism. They are essentially catholics (with a small "c") because, unlike some churches that also use the name Christian,[15] Protestant churches accept the Trinity, as well as other distinctively Catholic traits.

These functionally catholic Christians actively *protest* various teachings and practices of the Roman Catholic Church, hence the name Protest-ant. Some Protestants prefer to be called Reformed, Evangelical or "born again" Christians. Others just prefer to be labeled according to their denomination. (The term "Protestant" itself is simply a descriptive way to refer to all of them and is in no way intended as a pejorative in this book.) They all accept the Trinitarian definition of God. They worship Jesus Christ as God the Son. They use a New Testament that was compiled and canonized by the Catholic Church sixteen-hundred years ago (see Chapter 3). They celebrate Christian feasts (Christmas, Easter, All Hallows Eve, Saint Patrick's Day &

[15] These include; Jehovah's Witness, Christian Science, and the Church of Jesus Christ of Latter Day Saints, just to name a few.

Saint Valentine's Day) according to the Roman Catholic liturgical calendar.[16] They follow the Catholic practice of worshipping on Sundays. They arrange their churches with pews, an elevated sanctuary and occasionally an altar. All of these are essentially Roman Catholic traits. They've even retained some traditional Catholic hymns in some cases.

What makes them different is their rejection of Catholic authority, and some Catholic traditions, which they pick and choose as they see fit. Some Protestants, like the Anglicans for example, follow Catholic tradition quite closely, minus full submission to the authority of the pope of course. Other Protestants, like Seventh Day Adventists[17] for example, reject just about every Catholic tradition they can, including worship on Sundays. Most other Protestant denominations fall somewhere in between. If Catholicism is a "cult," then so is every Protestant church in the world.

No, Catholicism is not a "cult." We believe in the same God as Protestants and we don't engage in cult-like methods of deception and mind control. The Catholic Church is very transparent about its teachings and what it expects of its members. Some people may not like those

[16] Eastern Christians use a completely different liturgical calendar, marking different dates for Christmas and Easter, as well as different Saint days. While Protestants continue to cling to the Western calendar, formulated by the Roman Catholic Church, for the celebration of these holidays.

[17] Contrary to popular belief, the Seventh Day Adventists still accept the doctrine of the Trinity and the divinity of Jesus Christ, in spite of their affinity toward Sabbath keeping. So while many SDA Christians have a very negative opinion of the Catholic Church, they still cling to core Trinitarian catholic dogma.

teachings, for various reasons, but everyone knows exactly what they are.

Do some Catholic practices have Pagan origin?

This is highly unlikely even though that accusation has been repeatedly made over the last two centuries. In fact, it's been said so much, by so many different people, that it's often just accepted as "fact," even by some Catholics! Many of the so-called "Pagan" practices of Catholicism actually come from ancient Judaism, not Paganism, and in particular the Temple ceremonies of the ancient Jewish religion, coupled with common synagogue practices from the first century.

For example, when Catholics burn incense, it's sometimes thought to be of Pagan origin, but it was actually a common practice in the Jewish Temple period and commanded by God.[18] This custom was transferred to the New Testament era in St. John's revelation of pure heavenly worship.[19] Thus in imitation of pure heavenly worship, and the ancient Jewish worship of God, Catholic priests will typically burn incense around the altar within a Catholic church.

Another common accusation is that Sunday was used to worship the Pagan sun idol. Thus, it is said, Catholics transferred worship from Saturday (Sabbath) to Sunday, so as to accommodate Pagan converts. Actually, that is false. The institution of Sunday, as the designated Christian day of worship, was put into place by the Apostles

[18] Exodus 30:8

[19] Revelation 5:8

[20] and was called the "Lord's Day" in Scripture.[21] This was done in recognition of Jesus' resurrection on a Sunday, or the "*first day of the week.*" – (John 20:1)

Yet another extremely common accusation is that the celebration of Christmas comes from the Pagan feast of the winter solstice and that the Catholic Church simply absorbed this practice to again accommodate Pagan sun-worshippers. These accusations seem to have originated in the middle nineteenth century and offer no definitive proof of their validity. Most history scholars have now debunked the "Pagan-origin theory" of Christmas even though it is still widely accepted by the general population. A deeper investigation into the ancient Roman sun-cult revealed that its holiest day was on August 9th, and that Roman sun-worshippers ironically did not observe the equinoxes and solstices. On the other hand, two other things were going on at that time.

First, the Roman Jews, who followed Jesus as the Messiah, were put out of the synagogues (excommunicated from Judaism) in the late first century. Thus, they no longer had access to the Jewish calendar. The Jewish feast of Hanukkah always fell on the 25th day of the Jewish month of Kislev. However, without access to that calendar or the synagogue, it became difficult to calculate the proper day for this celebration which had great cultural significance to Jewish people. This was especially true for Jewish Christians, who commemorated Jesus' celebration of the feast recorded in John 10:22-23. Since the Jewish month of Kislev most commonly overlaps with the Julian month of

[20] Acts 20:7

[21] Revelation 1:10

December, it is believed many of these Jewish Christians in Rome celebrated their Christianized version of Hanukkah on December 25th instead, which usually falls close to Kislev 25th. Just as regular Jews celebrated the light that came into the Temple during this feast, so Christian Jews in Rome celebrated Jesus, the Light of God, who came into the same Temple during this feast. This Jewish-Christian Hanukkah, being an eight-day festival, with its conclusion on January 1st, eventually came to be known as the "Christmas Octave," on the Roman Catholic liturgical calendar.

Second, December 25th later came to be associated with the birth of Christ due to an earlier commemoration of his conception. This Feast of the Annunciation came to be celebrated on March 25th (which also came from another, completely different, Jewish custom),[22] that is exactly nine months before December 25th. Now all of this is just liturgical commemoration. Jesus didn't really need to be born on that literal date for us to celebrate it as his birthday, though there is considerable evidence that he was.

Still, that doesn't stop some groups from using this as a straw-man to attack the Catholic Church's celebration of Christmas. As ancient Christians in Rome increasingly marked December 25th as a holy day, the Pagan Roman emperor created the Feast of *Sol Invictus* (The Unconquered Sun) on December 25th in AD 274. He allegedly did this in an attempt to unite Christians and Pagans in the empire

[22] Integral Age: An ancient Jewish custom wherein it was believed that great prophets were conceived or born on the same date as their death. Since at that time it was believed that Jesus died on March 25th (according to the inaccurate Julian calendar), that date came to be associated with his conception as well.

under a common date for their religious celebrations. If indeed that was his intention, it turned out to be a miserable failure, as both *Sol Invictus*, and the Roman sun-cult, died out within a couple centuries.

No, it is not Catholicism that adopted Pagan dates and practices, but rather it is much more likely the other way around. The evidence seems to suggest that it was the Pagans, who in the twilight of their glory days, desperately tried to adopt Christian dates and practices to revive their dying cults. There are, of course, many more false accusations of crypto-Paganism within the Catholic Church, but the above demonstrates that these can be easily refuted with a little knowledge of history, religion and culture.

Must a person understand Latin to be a Catholic?

No. While Latin is the historical language of the Roman Catholic Church in the Western world, and it is helpful to know a little Latin, it's by no means required. While the Church has always retained its celebration of the ancient Latin liturgy,[23] it has in recent decades translated all of its liturgies into many vernacular languages. Today, people should have no problem finding a Catholic liturgy celebrated in their own spoken tongue.

That being said, even the Latin liturgies make accommodations for people who don't know Latin. If one should happen to find oneself at a Latin liturgy, booklets are provided to easily follow along. Scripture passages are read,

[23] *Usus Antiquior* or the Extraordinary Form of the Latin Rite

or re-read, in the vernacular language, and the homily (sermon) is always geven in the vernacular language as well.

Is the Catholic Church opposed to modern science?

No. Quite to the contrary, the Catholic Church virtually invented the scientific method! The Church has sponsored and blessed scientific research, and the Church embraces many scientific theories. Many Catholic priests actually have college degrees in science! In fact, the modern "big bang" theory of astro-physics, on the origin of the universe, was invented by a Catholic priest,[24] who was in good standing with the Church. However, the Catholic Church doesn't teach science as if it were religious doctrine. Rather it insists that science, like all human disciplines, must be subject to a moral code.[25] Catholics are free to believe in evolution as well, if they so choose, so long as they understand that it was God who created man in his image, and that human beings, and the universe we live in, are not a product of random chance. The idea being that whatever scientific processes God used to create the universe and man are open for debate. What is not open for debate is the religious truth that God created all things and that man was created in God's image.

[24] Father Georges Lemaître (1894 - 1966)

[25] Catechism of the Catholic Church, paragraph 2293

Why is Catholic worship so organized and structured compared to most Protestant worship?

Catholic worship is based in liturgy, and this liturgy comes primarily from ancient Jewish worship, both in the Temple and synagogues, and from the Biblical revelation that God is worshipped in heaven through liturgy.[26] The word "liturgy" is a Biblical word[27] and comes from a Greek composite word *leitourgia* (λειτουργία) meaning "the duty [or work] of the people." This is the prescribed method of public worship God gave to the Hebrew people in their Temple rites which was carried over into the synagogues. The celebrant recites a passage of Scripture, and the people respond with Scripture, or else a response based on Scripture.

The idea is to present an organized and dignified way through which people can express their personal relationship with God publicly and in community. For God has made the New Covenant in Christ with his Church, not the individual.[28] Individuals share in that covenant by becoming part of the larger Community (the Church) with which that covenant was made. The liturgy is merely a public expression of this. The Catholic Church has many liturgical rituals, but the two main rituals are the Divine Liturgy (often called the "Holy Mass") in which Holy

[26] Images of heavenly worship from the Book of Revelation

[27] Luke 1:23; Acts 13:2; Romans 15:16; 2nd Corinthians 9:12; Philippians 2:14-17, 25, 30; Hebrews 8:2 & 6

[28] Matthew 26:28; Luke 1:72; Romans 11:27; Hebrews 8:8; Hebrews 8:10; Hebrews 10:16

Communion is celebrated, and the Divine Office (also called the "Liturgy of the Hours") which is a recitation of the Psalms modeled after Jewish temple worship.

The Divine Office is the official prayer liturgy of the Catholic Church and it is required daily reading for clergy. Regular Catholics (laity) may optionally participate in it too. This Divine Office comes to us directly from the Temple prayer liturgy in ancient Israel, and is based heavily on the Psalms of David. Prayers are set aside for certain times of the day, and the Bible tells us about the Apostles going up to the Temple to pray this liturgy at certain times of the day.[29]

The Divine Liturgy (Holy Mass) is the official celebration of the Church, and it's obligatory for all Catholics on every Sunday and certain holy days during the year. This Divine Liturgy (Holy Mass) is a composite of two Jewish liturgies. The first half is the Liturgy of the Word, which comes to Catholicism directly from the Jewish synagogue liturgy. The second half is the Liturgy of the Eucharist, and this comes to us from the Jewish Passover seder combined with prayers used by Jewish priests in the ancient Temple period. Together, the Liturgy of the Word leads us into the Liturgy of the Eucharist. The whole thing marks a continuity between the Church and ancient Israel.

In contrast, when Protestants broke with the Catholic Church in the sixteenth century, they modified their liturgy accordingly. Anglicans and Lutherans initially made very little modifications. In contrast, Reformed and Anabaptists made rather large changes. As we go down through history we reach the modern Evangelical churches. They have stripped away a great deal of liturgy from their

[29] Acts 3:1

weekly services. However, they still retain a shell of liturgy. For example; certain times are designated for singing, other times for praying, and still another time for instruction. At various points during this liturgical shell, the congregation will stand up or sit down. While this is obviously less regimented and structured than Catholic liturgy, it is a shell of liturgy nonetheless.

Why is the Catholic Church so rich when so many of its members are poor?

That depends on what you mean by "rich." The accusation is levelled that the Catholic Church hoards money while it lets its members starve, and that such dire poverty is not seen in nations where Protestantism is the majority religion. The implication here is that Catholic countries are inherently "poor," while Protestant countries tend to be more affluent, and this somehow represents the "truthfulness" of Protestantism. Of course, said accusations fail to recognize the influence of godless Marxism in some of these poorer countries, but that's another topic.

First and foremost, let's get a few things straight. The Catholic Church is not "rich." It's the largest charitable organization in the world; feeding, sheltering and clothing more people than any other. It's also the largest provider of free educational and medical services on the planet. If you want to say the Catholic Church is "rich" in that it has a lot of resources to draw upon, that is one thing, but to say it hordes its money while letting its members languish in poverty is completely and totally false.

Priests and bishops usually take vows of poverty, which means they get paid a very meager salary, and usually own very few possessions. They usually live in very humble apartments or share houses with other clergy.

As for the instruments and edifices of Catholic worship; such as beautiful altars, vestments, silverware, shrines and massive basilicas, we must remember that these were donated by the people, specifically for the purpose of worship. This is because, in spite of their economic state in life, they *want to* worship God in a dignified way fitting for the Divine King Jesus. Thus, these things are dedicated to God alone. Priests and bishops do not "own" them. They belong to God, and they are donated to him by the people. This is absolutely Biblical when we consider the Old Testament descriptions of Temple worship during ancient times.

It's more than that however, unlike many Protestant churches, which are based primarily in the rich industrialized world, the Catholic Church is truly a universal Church, which is primarily based in the developing third-world. Thus, the Catholic Church is truly a Church of the poor. That being said, she champions the rights of the poor, which consist of many things, but one of those rights is the right to worship God in the same way the rich would, showing no distinction or partiality between rich and poor. We see this same advocating for the poor in the Temple worship of the Jews during ancient times.[30] The rich would bring their lambs and oxen for sacrifice, while the poor brought their pigeons and turtle-doves, or just flour in cases of extreme poverty, but the priest would show no partiality between them. Everyone offered their sacrifices equally in the same glorious Temple of marble and gold, which was dedicated

[30] Leviticus 5:11

exclusively to God for use by everyone. A similar mentality holds true in the Catholic Church. The poor may be poor, but that does not prohibit them from being brought into the "palace" of King Jesus – a Catholic parish or basilica. It is, after all, just as much for them as for the rich and middle class.

It's a common assumption, and a false one, that the Catholic Church hordes money because of the beautiful instruments and edifices of Catholic worship. Such assumptions only illustrate a lack of understanding of what these things are for, and a lack of understanding of how the Catholic Church uses the overwhelming vast majority of its resources to help the poor.

Many Christians believe all sins are equal, do Catholics believe this too?

No. The Catholic Church teaches that there are two different kinds of sins: mortal and venial.[31] This is because the Scriptures tell us there are two types of sin: one that leads unto death (mortal), and one that does not lead unto death (venial).[32]

Many sins are habitual, or don't constitute a serious matter, or don't involve the full consent of the will. These sins are considered "venial," which means they do not lead to spiritual death. They may not break our relationship with God, but they do harm our relationship with God. Consequently, Catholics may continue to receive communion, and remain in good standing with the Church,

[31] Catechism of the Catholic Church, paragraphs 1854-1864
[32] 1st John 5:16

even when they've committed venial sin. However, they should seek to confess and repent of these sins whenever possible, because they can easily lead to mortal sin when left unchecked.

Some sins are very serious, involve a serious matter, and do involve the full consent of the will. In these cases, the sin is called mortal, because it does break our relationship with God. A mortal sin can lead to death, and by that is meant spiritual death. The soul in a state of mortal sin is in danger of hell. When one is in a state of mortal sin, one is not in good standing with the Church, and should not present one's self for communion. Confession and repentance of all known mortal sins are necessary for salvation, and to return into a right relationship with God (a state of grace), and to restore a good standing in the Church.

What is the Catholic Church's position on sexual sin?

The Catholic Church's position on sexual sin is pretty basic and simple. Sexual relations, of all kinds, are forbiddon, except between an adult married couple: one biological male and one biological female.[33] This puts a whole lot of popular sexual activity outside of what the Catholic Church permits as lawful.

The following sexual activities are examples of sexual sin according to Catholic teaching: lust, voyeurism, masterbation, contraception, fornication, homosexuality, polygamy, polyamory, pederasty, pedophilia, rape, sodomy, bestiality, etc. All of these sexual activities are considered

[33] Catechism of the Catholic Church, paragraphs 2337, 2350-2363

unlawful, according to Catholic teaching, regardless of what is allowed by civil law, requiring confession and repentance. The degree of sin can vary, whether mortal or venial, depending on the type and circumstances. However, these activities are always considered sinful.

That being said, the temptation to commit sexual sin (of any kind) is not a sin, and temptation (in and of itself) is not sinful. We know this because Jesus Christ was tempted to sin,[34] even though he never committed any sin.[35] Thus, temptation and sin are two different things. Wanting to do something is not the same as doing it. The sin is in the doing, not the wanting, but we should examine *why* we want things that are sinful. More often than not, passing desires to commit sin (temptations) are rooted in misbeliefs, lies or sources outside ourselves. So merely having a passing desire to commit a sexual sin (sexual temptation) does not constitute sin (in itself) according to Catholic teaching. When it comes to sexual sin, the action is what counts, not the temptation.

If, however, one is subjected to constant temptation, one should try to discover the reasons why. Sometimes our own actions or misbeliefs can make us more vulnerable to unnecessary trials.

Lust, for example, is a sin committed primarily in the mind. The Catechism defines it as "*disordered desire for or inordinate enjoyment of sexual pleasure*" that is rooted in pleasure in itself, for pleasure's sake, without the unitive or procreative purposes it was designed for.[36] Lust is rooted in

[34] Mark 1:13; Luke 4:1-13

[35] Hebrews 4:15

[36] Catechism of the Catholic Church, paragraph 2351

the misbelief that sexual activity is primarily for personal entertainment, and really doesn't have much meaning beyond that. When this misbelief is corrected, the temptation to lust is greatly reduced.

What is the Catholic Church's position on abortion?

The Catholic Church teaches that abortion is the murder of innocent human life: always, all the time, no excetions.[37] This is a mortal sin, and those who procure an abortion are automatically excommunicated from the Catholic Church.[38] This means everyone involved in the process, not just the mother and abortionist. It also includes everyone who works at the abortion clinic, the husband/boyfriend who drove the mother in for the appointment, the person who knowingly consented to pay for the procedure, the political activist who lobbied to legalize the procedure, the judge who legalized the procedure in court, and the politician who voted to keep the procedure legal. This applies to all persons at least sixteen years of age.[39] In fact, the United States Conference of Catholic Bishops (USCCB), by no means a politically conservative body, has explicitly stated that it is impossible to be pro-abortion (pro-choice) and remain Catholic.[40]

However, medical procedures, designed to save the life of the mother, do not qualify as an abortion, so long as

---

[37] Catechism of the Catholic Church, paragraphs 2270-2275

[38] Code of Canon Law 1398

[39] Code of Canon Law 1323, 1325

[40] National Council of Catholic Bishops, Fall 1989 conference resolution of November 8, 1989

there is no *intent* to kill the unborn child. This is called the "principle of double effect."[41] The death of the unborn child may be the unintended result of the procedure, with both the doctor and patient knowing this in advance. So long as the desire to kill the baby (or terminate the pregnancy) is not present in such a medically-necessary procedure, it is not an abortion, nor is it murder, even if both the doctor and patient know that termination of the pregnancy will be the likely result. Such rare circumstances qualify as "double effect" because both lives (baby and mother) are equally valuable, and losing both would be a greater evil than losing one. "*If medical treatment or surgical operation, necessary to save a mother's life, is applied to her organism (though the child's death would, or at least might, follow as a regretted but unavoidable consequence), it should not be maintained that the fetal life is thereby directly attacked.*" – (Catholic Enclyclopia, Abortion, 1907)

What is the Catholic Church's position on artificial contraception?

As stated above, the purpose of sex is both unitive and procreative within the context of marriage.[42] According to Catholic teaching, sex has to serve these two purposes, within marriage, to be lawful. This is why the Catholic Church opposes all forms of artificial contraception.[43]

We have to stop and think about what sex is for. It's not always for making babies. That's only half of the reason, but is it half! Obviously, God doesn't expect a wife to

[41] Catechism of the Catholic Church, paragraphs 1752, 1754, 1756, 1759

[42] Catechism of the Catholic Church, paragraph 2351

[43] Catechism of the Catholic Church, paragraphs 2370 & 2399

become pregnant with every conjugal act, and God does allow natural means in which spouses can space their children and still enjoy the regular unitive half of lawful sex within marriage. Likewise, spouses who experience infertility due to advanced age, or some other reason, may still experience the unitive half of sexual relations, which is blessed by God both in natural law and Church law. This isn't about circumstances beyond human control. This is specifically about human beings taking too much control.

The whole biological purpose of sex is procreation, and from a purely biological perspective in natural law, that is its sole fuction. The pleasure that human beings derive from the conjugal act is an additional blessing from God that helps spouses strengthen the intimacy of their relationship. In other words, it helps improve their lifelong bond with each other. That's why humans experience it. It may be the only reason why humans experience it, purely as a blessing from God. Creatures of the animal kingdom are not so blessed. They procreate by instinct and, for them, it's not usually a pleasurable experience. They only do it because instinct tells them they must.

God has created the female body with a cyclic regularity that allows fertile couples to time their conjugal acts with periodic continence, in a way the Church recognizes as lawful and responsible family planning. The Vatican made judgements on this in 1853, 1880 and 1932 through the Apostolic Penitentiary, a dicastry of the Roman Curia. The latter judgement, in 1932, came just after the publication of *Casti Connubii* in 1930, the papal encyclical of Pope Pius XI condemning artificial contraception. The teaching of Pius XI, against artificial contraception, was reaffirmed by Pope Paul VI's 1968 encyclical *Humanae Vitae.* This encyclical specifically restates what the Church had already decided through the decisions of the Apostolic Penitentiary. "*Neither the Church nor her doctrine is inconsistent when she considers it lawful for married people to take advantage of the infertile period...*"[44] This is again reaffirmed in the Catechism.[45]

Catholic married couples, who are fertile, are expected to use a process called "Natural Family Planning," or NFP, if they wish to space their children and plan their family accordingly. Recent scientific and medical advances, which help spouses understand the thermo-symptomatic cycle of the female body, have made this method of spacing children highly reliable, even more reliable than most methods of artificial contraception. Scientific/medical advances, combined with modern technology, now make it possible for married couples to practice this effectively, and conveniently, producing reliable family planning without foreign devices or chemical hormones. All a married couple needs now is a thermometer, a smartphone, a little training and discipline. Truly, we are living in remarkable times.

What many of today's Christians don't understand is that all Christian denominations considered artificial contraception to be a grave sin, all the way up to 1930. All of the original Protestant Reformers condemned it, along with the founders of major Protestant denominations, including Martin Luther, John Calvin and John Wesley.[46] It was the Anglicans who opened the door to artificial

[44] Pope Paul VI, *Humanae Vitae*, 16

[45] Catechism of the Catholic Church, paragraph 2368

[46] As quoted by Charles D. Provan, *The Bible and Birth Control*, 1989

contraception in the 1930 Lambeth Conference. From there, the entire Protestant world caved in the decades that followed. Only the Catholic Church held the line, defending the ancient Christian teaching against it.

The Biblical prohibition against artificial contraception is in Genesis 38:8-10. This is backed by the early Church Fathers who likewise interpreted artificial contraception as a grave sin.[47] The problem here is that artificial contraception, meaning an unnatural method of preventing pregnancy, completely closes off the procreative half of the conjugal act, reducing sex to mere entertainment for pleasure's sake, otherwise known as lust. Unlike NFP, fertile spouses no longer remain open to the creation of life at all. They are attempting to have sex, while cutting out all possible means of creating children, when God has clearly given them those natural means through their fertility. The problem that results is this. What happens when contraception fails? All too often, couples will turn to abortion, because with contraception, they were never open to the possibility of new life to begin with.

Ultimately, this is about playing God to indulge in sexual pleasure. God has already given fertile spouses everything they need to plan their family reasonably. In failing to trust God, however, and the natural processes he created, the married couple has taken matters into their own hands, in a very unnatural, artificial, harmful and sinful way.

[47] Clement of Alexandria, *The Instructor of Children* 2:10:91:2 (AD 195); Hippolytus of Rome, *Refutation of All Heresies* 9:12 (AD 255); Lactantius, *Divine Institutes* 6:20 (AD 307); St Augustine of Hippo, Marriage and Concupiscence 1:15:17 (AD 419)

Are Catholics socialists?

No. At least, we're not supposed to be. Officially speaking, the Catholic Church does not prescribe or recommend any particular economic system, but rather sits in judgement of them all, based on the teachings of the gospel. While the Church has been critical of capitalism, it has never condemned the capitalist system outright. However, in regards to the economic philosophy of Karl Marx and Friedrich Engels (Marxism, socialism and communism), the Church has made outright condemnations of that.[48] Catholics cannot be Marxists, socialists or communists. Not even so-called "democratic socialism" is permitted for Catholics.

The problem centers around private property, and the right of every human being to own it, which the Catholic Church fully recognizes. Marxism condemns this right. Socialism restricts it. While communism forbids it.

The Catholic Church recognizes that every person has the right to acquire private property (house, land, cattle, tools, business, etc.) and use it as a means to provide for one's self and family. Marxism, on the other hand, encourages the sin of covetousness ("class envy" or "class warfare"), violating the Tenth Commandment,[49] condemning the ownership of private property. Socialism is Marxism-in-action, working to restrict the ownership of

[48] Pope Leo XIII, *Rerum Novarum* 4, 5, 14, 15, 17; Pope John XXIII, *Mater et Magistra* 34; Pope Paul VI, *Octogesima Adveniens* 31; Pope St John Paul II, *Centesimus Annus* 12

[49] Tenth Commandment: "You shall not covet your neighbor's goods."

private property, and is therefore unjust, legally validating theft, a violation of the Seventh Commandment.[50] Communism, which is ultimate-socialism-in-action, forbides the ownership of all private property, making theft and covetousness the foundation of society, turning the whole Ten Commandments upside-down.

When we combine this with the bizarre sexual ideology of Marxism, a violation of the Sixth Commandment,[51] which seeks to abolish the traditional family,[52] and the Marxist notion that children should become wards of communities rather than parents, we have a socio-economic system that is antithetical to everything the Catholic Church teaches. This is why we have over a century of papal encyclicals and statements condemning the ideology of Marx and Engels. No Catholic can subscribe to it and still call himself a Catholic in good standing.

Are all Catholics the same?

No. While there are different types of Catholics, both liturgically and culturally, all Catholics are supposed to follow the same beliefs (doctrines) and moral code. Unlike other Christians, doctrinal beliefs do not change from parish to parish within the Catholic Church. All Catholics are supposed to follow the same beliefs and morals.

That being said, not all Catholics follow the same beliefs and morals equally. Some strive very hard to live as good and faithful Catholics, in accordance with Church

---

[50] Seventh Commandment: "You shall not steal."

[51] Sixth Commandment: "You shall not commit adultery."

[52] Communist Manifesto, chapter 2, page 24

teaching. Others may not strive nearly as hard. Those Catholics who consistently show a pattern of failing to adhere to the Church's doctrinal teachings, and/or its moral code, are called *Lapsed* Catholics.

Most of the time, being a Lapsed Catholic is a private matter, usually known only by God, the sinner and the priest in the confessional. The Catholic Church takes great care to safeguard the privacy of personal sins, and generally does not make public statements about a particular Lapsed Catholic.

On rare occasions, however, Lapsed Catholics can be public figures, whose scandalous behavior becomes a source of public confusion. For example, sometimes a Lapsed Catholic may be a celebrity or politician, who might give the appearance that the Catholic Church condones certain heresies (false teachings) and/or sinful behavior. When this happens, said Lapsed Catholic is supposed to be corrected by his bishop, and he is supposed to be denied communion by the priests until he publicly repents of the publicly scandalous behavior. Sadly, however, it is possible for clergy to be lapsed as well. When a Lapsed Catholic, who is a celebrity or politician, is enabled by a lapsed bishop who refuses to perform the duties of his vocation, it becomes a source of great public scandal that bismerches the reputation of the entire Catholic Church.

It should be noted that when such situations occur, they are not the result of authentic Catholic teaching, but rather the failure of individual sinners. The failure of Judas Iscariot was not the result of Jesus' teaching. It was, rather, in spite of it. Since the time of the Apostles, the Catholic

Church has always had lapsed members. Jesus warned us this would always be so, until his Second Coming on the Last Day.[53]

In contrast, a *Practicing* Catholic is one who tries to faithfully follow the teachings and morals of the Church, in practice, in spite of personal failings that are confessed and repented of. Nobody's perfect. All Catholics sin. All Catholics have misbeliefs from time to time. So long as Catholics are seeking to follow the teachings of the Church, and remain open to correction, confession and repentance, they remain Practicing Catholics. So in the end, while there are many different types of rites, forms and jurisdictions in the Catholic Church, giving the Church her rich diversity, there are only two types of Catholics in practical application: practicing and lapsed.

[53] Matthew 13:24-30, 36-43

CHAPTER 2: SPECIFIC QUESTIONS

Why do Catholics call priests "father" when the Bible says "call no man father?"

The passage that some use to support the idea that Catholics shouldn't call a priest "father" is found in Matthew 23:9 wherein Jesus commanded his followers to call no man "teacher" or "father." This passage is commonly cited against the Catholic practice of calling priests "father." However, when we look at this passage in context, we see that Jesus is not prohibiting the use of the word "father" but rather rebuking religious leaders who do not serve their people as a father serves his family. He is rebuking the Pharisees of his time because they were called "rabbi" (which literally means "teacher" or "great one") and accepted the religious honor without embracing the sacrifice and humility that is supposed to go along with it. Jesus was commanding his disciples (later Apostles) to not be like that. He didn't want them to think they were greater than the people they were shepherding. He wanted them to think of themselves as servants of the people. The same goes for religious leaders today.

Clearly the titles of "rabbi" and "father" are not prohibited in and of themselves. Jesus accepted the title of "rabbi" on many occasions. Jesus called Abraham "father." [54] St Stephen called the Jewish leaders "fathers" just before

[54] Matthew 3:9

he was martyred by them.[55] Are we to believe that St Stephen disobeyed Jesus by calling men "father" just before he was martyred? St Paul also called the Jewish leaders "fathers."[56] Are we to believe St Paul was disobeying Jesus Christ by doing this? St Paul also refers to St Timothy as his "*beloved* ***<u>son</u>*** *in faith.*" – (1st Timothy 1:2)[57] If Timothy is a "son" in the faith, then what do we suppose Timothy called St Paul in the faith? St Paul specifically told the Corinthian Christians that he *"became"* their *"father in Christ Jesus through the gospel."* – (1st Corinthians 4:14-15)[58] He said the same to his disciple Philemon.[59]

When we read the writings of the early Christians of the first few centuries, it becomes clear that the practice of referring to Christian leaders as "father" was commonplace. This is because the early Christians understood Jesus' prohibition on the use of the title "father" in its appropriate context. Jesus was addressing arrogance in leadership. He was not prohibiting the use of certain titles. We Catholics call our priests "father" because that's how we look at them. We see them as paternal guardians of our parish family. They serve the role of a "father" in this spiritual setting. In Catholic Christianity, we look at the Church as one big family. We address priests as "fathers," nuns as "sisters" and monks as "brothers." We don't do this because *we* think they are somehow superior, nor do *they* think they are

[55] Acts 7:2

[56] Acts 21:40; Acts 22:1

[57] Emphasis mine

[58] Revised Standard Version Catholic Edition (RSVCE)

[59] Philemon 10

superior. Rather, we do it simply as a sign of family affection.

Why do Catholics confess their sins to a priest when they could go directly to God?

We confess our sins to a priest because Jesus told us to. You see, while Jesus was on earth he regularly forgave people's sins. The religious leaders of his time were indignant about this, asking: "*Who can forgive sins, but God only?*" – (Mark 2:7) Jesus received some really harsh judgement from the religious leaders of his time over this. However, he proved to them that he did indeed have the authority to forgive sins by doing miracles that only God could do. No Christian today denies that Jesus has the authority to forgive sins.[60] That's beyond dispute now. Catholics however, take the whole testimony of Scripture into account.

Not only did Jesus have the authority to forgive sins, but he also shared this authority with his Apostles and their successors: *"He said therefore to them again: Peace be to you. As the Father hath sent me, I also send you. When he had said this, he breathed on them; and he said to them: Receive ye the Holy Ghost. Whose sins you shall forgive, they are forgiven them; and whose sins you shall retain, they are retained."* – (John 20:21-23) This one passage alone demonstrates, beyond the shadow of a doubt, that Jesus shared his authority to forgive (and retain) sins

[60] Matthew 9:2-8

with his Apostles. The Apostles then hand-picked their own successors[61] and likewise transferred this ministry to them.[62]

For Catholics, this is simply a matter of believing the Bible and taking what it says seriously. Either Jesus gave some men his authority to forgive sins, or he did not, and the Bible clearly says he did.

Now when we Catholics commit a sin, we do confess those sins directly to God, both before confession and during confession. The priest then, by the authority he has based on Jesus' own words, dispenses Christ's forgiveness in an official way, as if Jesus Christ himself had said it.

The real question here is not why do Catholics go to a priest? But rather, why do other Christians ***not*** go to a priest when the Bible specifically says that Jesus gave some men the authority to forgive sins in his place? Since the earliest days of the Church, Christians have always approached their church leaders for absolution. What makes some Christians today think they're so different? Catholics don't see any difference at all. The early Christians approached their church leaders for reconciliation. So do we.

Why can't Catholic priests be married?

Actually, they can be married. That's a big secret you see. With special papal permission, any celibate Catholic priest can give up the priesthood to have a wife and family,[63]

---

[61] Acts 1:20-26

[62] 2nd Corinthians 5:17-20

[63] Code of Canon Law: 291

and since all of them are fairly well-educated men, with college degrees, they'll have no problem picking up good secular jobs or starting family businesses.

Nuns and monks are the same way. They can, at any time, choose to leave their orders to pursue a secular life in holy matrimony. Most of them are highly educated too. Nobody is a "prisoner" of his or her religious vocation.

I say this only because I've actually heard some people suggest that Catholic clergy, as well as nuns and monks, are "prisoners" of their religious vows, and could never get married. Nothing could be further from the truth. These men, and women, choose celibacy voluntarily. Nobody coerced them into it. They can leave it all behind too, and pursue a married life. Their choice to remain celibate is a prophetic sign for the rest of us to see. There are greater things in this world than sex, and nobody has sex in the afterlife anyway.[64] Their celibacy in this world points to their anticipation of the next.

There is another secret. It is possible for a Catholic priest to be both a priest and married at the same time. In fact, there are thousands of married Catholic priests who are active in the priesthood. You see, the required vow of clerical celibacy is a discipline not a doctrine, and it only applies to the Latin Rite of the Catholic Church. There are seven rites that make up the Catholic Church. A "rite" is a particular way of being Catholic. Each rite has its own liturgy, tradition and disciplines. Some of these rites have their own juridical churches, and sub-rites associated with them. All of them are part of the larger Catholic Church and are in full communion with the pope in Rome. According to

[64] Matthew 22:30

the Catechism, the seven liturgical rites of the Catholic Church are: Latin, Byzantine, Alexandrian, Syriac, Armenian, Maronite, and Chaldean.[65] The Latin Rite (also called the "Roman Rite") is just one of these seven rites, but it is the largest, and it is the most well known. Married men are permitted to become Catholic priests in six of these seven rites.[66] In spite of that, however, many of these men choose celibacy instead. We don't see much of these other six rites in the Western world except in big cities. In the Eastern world however, they are quite common.

Only the Latin Rite strictly ordains celibate men to the priesthood, and even then, there are exceptions to this rule. For example, if married Protestant ministers wish to convert to Catholicism and become Catholic priests, the Latin Rite has been known to allow them to do this on a case-by-case basis.[67] There are also the Personal Ordinariates of English Patrimony within the Latin Rite, which permit this exception on a much larger scale, mainly for former Anglican and Methodist clergymen.[68]

The discipline of mandating clerical celibacy, strictly within the Latin Rite, was instituted during the latter Middle Ages for very practical reasons. It can be changed at any time. That being said, as of the date of this writing, there is no indication the pope plans to change it anytime soon. A celibate priesthood has worked well for the Latin Rite, ensuring its rapid growth around the world.

---

[65] Catechism of the Catholic Church, paragraph 1203

[66] Catechism of the Catholic Church, paragraph 1580

[67] *Sacerdotalis coelibatus*, 42

[68] *Anglicanorum coetibus,* VI. 1-2

The idea of clerical celibacy is Biblical. Jesus was celibate and he praised those who chose a celibate life to serve the Kingdom of God.[69] St Paul, who was also celibate, actually recommended celibacy for anyone working in full-time ministry.[70] The vow of celibacy among women in the Church (early nuns) was even commonplace in the Apostolic era while St Paul was still writing the New Testament.[71]

In response to the recent growing interest of married Catholic men entering ministry, the Latin Rite of the Catholic Church has also reopened the position of the permanent diaconate for married Catholic men who feel such a calling. The diaconate allows married Catholic men to become deacons in the Catholic Church.[72]

Now a Catholic deacon has a lot more authority than the typical Evangelical deacon. Catholic deacons work for the bishop, alongside priests (presbyters). They assist in the liturgies of the Church, they can preach homilies (sermons), teach the faith, minister to the sick, baptize the faithful and perform weddings. Basically a Catholic deacon can do just about anything an Evangelical pastor does, but without the trappings of having to run a church. (That's usually the priest's job.) The only thing a Catholic deacon does not do is celebrate the Eucharist, hear confessions and anoint the sick, but then, an Evangelical pastor cannot do these things either. At least, he can't from a Catholic perspective anyway. In many ways, a Catholic deacon is

[69] Matthew 19:12

[70] 1st Corinthians 7:32-35

[71] 1st Timothy 5:9-12

[72] Code of Canon Law: 1031.2

parallel to an Evangelical pastor in function and authority. The diaconate serves as an excellent way for married Catholic men to participate in the vocation of Church ministry in an official way. That is, if they are called to it of course.

Why does the Catholic Church not ordain women?

The Catholic Church does not ordain women for three reasons. First, it is strictly prohibited in Sacred Scripture. Second, it is strictly prohibited in Apostolic Tradition. Third, it is a distortion of the ministry of Jesus Christ.

First, Sacred Scripture forbids the ordination of women to any clerical state. The clerical offices of the Church are threefold: deacon, presbyter (priest) and bishop. In every case, along with many other qualifications, the Scriptures state that the candidate must be a man, and if he is married, he can only be the husband of one wife.[73] The Bible only recognizes two genders: biological male and biological female. Likewise, the Bible makes it very clear that marriage can only be between a biological male and a biological female. So if the Scriptures dictate that one prerequisite for the clerical state is to be the "husband" (biological male) of one wife (biological female), it's pretty plain to see the Scriptures insist on biological males for the clergy. That, and the fact that the Scriptures refer to such candidates as men and always use male pronouns.

[73] 1st Timothy 3:1-7; Titus 1:5-9

St Paul isn't the least bit shy about this. He insists, in no uncertain terms, that women cannot hold any positions of authority in the Church – ever.[74] He makes no exception about this. "*I permit no woman to teach or to have authority over men; she is to keep silent. For Adam was formed first, then Eve; and Adam was not deceived, but the woman was deceived and became a transgressor. Yet woman will be saved through bearing children, if she continues in faith and love and holiness, with modesty.*" – (1st Timothy 2:12-15)[75]

By today's politically-correct standards of speech, this sounds sexist. However, we have to understand that the ancients knew nothing of political correctness, and were quite blunt in their speech by today's standards. This text must be properly interpreted in context. The context of the passage is prayer, specifically public prayer in a church setting. Paul is talking about who leads prayer, and he references men here (clergy). The women he tells to "*keep silent.*" That doesn't mean they can't talk. What he's saying is they can't lead in prayer, meaning specifically, they can't officiate the liturgy. Of course, women can speak in church in other ways, in non-authoritative ways, such as: they can sing in choirs, make announcements, even read some passages of Scripture, etc. But women cannot officiate the liturgy. St Paul makes this clear by saying he does "*not permit a woman to teach or to have authority.*" That's the key word here – "authority." Officiating the liturgy is a sign of authority. That's why St Paul forbids it.

His explanation deserves some context as well. Otherwise, our politically-correct society will not tolerate it.

---

[74] 1st Corinthians 14:34

[75] Revised Standard Version Catholic Edition (RSVCE)

He references the story of Adam and Eve in the Old Testament in saying: *"Adam was not deceived, but the woman was deceived and became a transgressor."* This does not mean he's blaming the woman (Eve) for all the sins in the world. On the contrary, he's giving the woman (Eve) an excuse. He's saying the woman was deceived by the serpent (devil). She didn't fully understand what she was doing. One could derive from this that women are more easily deceived than men. Whether or not that's true is irrelevant, because that's not what St Paul is getting at here. What he's getting at is the woman (Eve) committed the lesser sin. She was deceived or tricked into doing it. The man (Adam), on the other hand, knew exactly what he was doing. The early Christians[76] understood the man (Adam) as committing the greater sin because he was not deceived. He chose, rather, to subordinate himself to his wife and follow her lead into sin, instead of being a spiritual leader and helping to guide her out of it.

This is part of St Paul's explanation for why God wants men to become spiritual leaders in the Church and their homes. It's necessary in the male path to salvation. The sin of the first man (Adam) must be corrected in every Christian man. Men must become spiritual leaders again, either in the Church or in their homes, self-sacrificial in character, if they hope to be what God intended them to become. In the Christian spiritual economy, leadership is not lordship. It's sacrifice, meaning the sacrifice of one's self for the betterment of others. Women do this almost naturally all the time. Men do not. That's part of the sin of Adam. St

[76] St Augustine of Hippo (AD 430), St Gregory of Nyssa (AD 394), St Ambrose of Milan (AD 397)

Paul corrects that here, by restricting Church leadership (clergy) to men alone.

We have to understand, St Paul wrote this at a time when the Church was persecuted in the Holy Land, and received sporadic persecution elsewhere. In time, it would soon receive the persecution of the entire Roman Empire. Christian leaders were the first to be taken during persecutions. Being a Christian leader meant not only sacrificing your personal life for the good of your congregation, but often sacrificing your physical life to protect your congregation. St Paul wants men to become self-sacrificing "fathers" in the Church.

The last portion deserving context is St Paul's second explanation: "*woman will be saved through bearing children.*" This does **not** mean women have to birth children to go to heaven! Rather, it means that a woman's place in spiritual leadership (leading prayer) is with children. By raising children in holiness, teaching them to follow Christ, Christian women undo the sin of Eve. Instead of being deceived by the devil, they can now prevent children from being deceived – any children, not just their own. When we understand the context of Paul's words here, we can begin to appreciate why he commanded the men to "man up" and lead through self-sacrifice in the Church and in their homes. As for women, he just tells them that they, and their leadership talents, are preserved (saved) through bringing children to Christ.

Second, Apostolic Tradition mirrors Sacred Scripture, both in the Apostolic Age and throughout the centuries. There is no credible evidence of women being ordained to the clerical state throughout the bimillennial history of the Church. The bottom line is this. If Jesus Christ intended women to be ordained, he had in his presence the most perfect, humble and worthy woman in all of history. That would be his own mother, Mary. Why didn't he ordain her? Let's face it. If Jesus Christ wouldn't even ordain Mary, then what gives anybody the notion that he would want to ordain less-worthy women today? Nobody (neither man nor woman) is more worthy than Mary.

Pope St John Paul II put it succinctly in his 1994 Apostolic Letter on the topic. In it, he wrote: "*Wherefore, in order that all doubt may be removed regarding a matter of great importance, a matter which pertains to the Church's divine constitution itself, in virtue of my ministry of confirming the brethren (Luke 22:32) I declare that the Church has no authority whatsoever to confer priestly ordination on women and that this judgment is to be definitively held by all the Church's faithful.*" – (Pope St. John Paul II, *Ordinatio sacerdotalis*, 4) The operative phrase here is "*the Church has no authority whatsoever.*" The Church cannot have any authority that Christ has not already given it. When it comes to ordaining clergy, Christ is our example. We cannot do more than he did. Jesus Christ only ordained men to the clerical state. He did not ordain women, children, or anyone else – only men. We could go as far as the example set by the Apostles, but no further. They only ordained men as well. To ordain women now, would be an innovation (making something up out of thin air), which the Church has no authority to do. Thus, any attempt to ordain a woman to the clerical state would be automatically invalid, null and void.

Third, this all comes down to the nature of the ministry of Jesus Christ. Being ordained (becoming clergy) means sharing in Christ's ministry. It is his ministry, not ours. It is his authority, not ours. It is his very nature, not ours. When the sacraments of the Church are administered, the administrator becomes *in persona Christi* (Latin: "in the person of Christ"). Jesus Christ is a man. He is not a woman. Nor is he without gender. When one is ordained to the clerical state, one shares in the ministry and nature of Christ – who is a man. The cleric becomes *in persona Christi* – representing the divine God-Man – to the flock he shepherds. A woman can be many things, but she can never be a man. Any attempt to do so is merely an illusion, for the XX chromosomal makeup of every cell in her body cries out: "I am a woman." Women cannot be ordained, for to be ordained is to share in the male ministry, male authority and male nature of Christ. Jesus Christ can be many things, but he can never be a woman.

Why do some Catholic women wear head-coverings in church?

The practice is truly old, and comes from ancient Judaism prior to the birth of Jesus Christ. During that time, many pious Jews (both men and women) would cover their heads during prayer. Modern Jews still practice this in their synagogues today. This is to show humility and subordination before God. The Old Testament did not command this of ancient Jews, as only the priests were required to cover their heads by Law,[77] but the custom developed in ancient Jewry and remains among many Jews to this day.

[77] Exodus 28:4,37,40

In the New Testament, however, St Paul pointed out that the early Church modified this practice, commanding men to uncover their heads during prayer, but that women should remain covered.[78] This was to emphasize the new order that Christ created through his incarnation, death and resurrection. In the Christian spiritual economy, men represent Christ and women represent the Church.

The Catholic Church added to this by veiling all things that are holy within the church. The holy chalice is veiled at certain parts of the liturgy. The tabernacle is traditionally veiled. Other items are sometimes veiled, most particularly those things that carry the presence of the Lord Jesus Christ. The veiling of women is likewise considered an act of veiling that which is holy. Women bear children in the tabernacle of their wombs, and this is in recognition of their physical likeness to the Blessed Virgin Mary, who bore the Son of God in her womb. It is notable that in sacred art, the Blessed Virgin Mary is almost always veiled.

This may seem foreign to some people in our post-feminist world, wherein headcoverings are wrongly seen as some kind of sign of subjection to a male patriarchy. It should be noted that in the Christian economy, women veil in the presence of God not men. If it had anything to do with male patriarchy, women would be required to veil before men at all times, especially in public, as we see in Islam. Such is not the case in Christianity.

Catholic women were at one time required to wear some type of a head-covering while inside a Catholic Church. This is no longer the case following the relaxation of canon law in 1983. Today, Catholic women do it

[78] 1st Corinthians 11:1-16

voluntarily, in accordance with Catholic tradition and Biblical teaching.

We still see remnants of this practice in our post-Christian society. During public prayer at sporting events, men often remove their hats while women do not. Brides are often veiled at weddings, but grooms are not. All of this comes from the practice of female head-covering, which was common throughout most Christian churches up until around 1970.

Are Catholics allowed to divorce?

The short answer is "no." The reason why is because Jesus Christ forbade his followers from dovorce, and the Catholic Church takes Jesus' teachings on marriage very seriously. Thus, Catholics are not allowed to divorce, and the Catholic Church does not recognize civil divorces. From the Catholic Church's perspective, the state does not have the authority to contract an actual marriage, nor does the state have the authority to dissolve one. All the state can do is handle legal matters: like marital rights, name changes, civil assets and child custody, etc.

This requires a little understanding about natural marriage and the sacrament of matrimony. For the sake of simplicity here, I'll just cover the sacrament of matrimony.

According to Catholic teaching, the "ministers" of matrimony are the bride and the groom, not the priest, pastor, judge or civil officer of any type. The bride gives herself in matrimony to the groom. The groom gives himself in matrimony to the bride. Thus, the ministers of the sacrament are the bride and groom. In a Catholic Church, the priest is just there to witness the sacrament on behalf of the whole Church. Practically speaking, he guides them through the process too, but it needs to be understood he is not "marrying them." They are marrying each other.

Since a priest does not "marry" couples, neither does a minister of any other religion, nor does an agent of the state. Couples marry each other. They don't need anyone to marry them. The only thing they need are witnesses. When it comes to a Catholic getting married, according to canon law, he or she must have a member of the Catholic clergy (bishop, priest or deacon) witness the wedding in order for the marriage to be valid, unless a bishop has given permission to do otherwise.[79]

Understanding this, let's move on to Jesus' teaching about divorce. Many Evangelicals point to Jesus' words in Matthew's gospel: "*And I say to you: whoever divorces his wife, except for unchastity, and marries another, commits adultery; and he who marries a divorced woman, commits adultery.*" – (Matthew 19:9)[80] Now this term in English, "unchastity" seems pretty broad. This causes many to think that Jesus permits divorce when a spouse is unfaithful. Wait, not so fast! The actual Greek word used here is *porneia* (πορνεία), which has more than one meaning. On the one hand, it could mean what is commonly thought by most Evangelicals: adultery, fornication, homosexuality, etc. On the other hand, however, there is a secondary meaning: sexual intercourse or "marriage" with close relatives. Such "marriages" are directly forbidden by the Mosaic Law of the Old Testament.[81]

[79] Code of Canon Law 1127.2

[80] Revised Standard Version Catholic Edition (RSVCE)

[81] Leviticus 18:1-18

If Matthew was using this secondary definition when he wrote this, then it would mean that the only time Jesus' followers could "divorce" is when the marriage was unlawful to begin with. Thus, it was null and void from the start. To help us find the meaning to Jesus' words, we must look beyond Matthew's gospel. In Mark's gospel, we read the parallel passage: "*Whoever divorces his wife and marries another, commits adultery against her; and if she divorces her husband and marries another, she commits adultery.*" – (Mark 10:11-12)[82] Here, Mark recorded the words of Jesus in a more plain and simple way. Jesus does not recognize divorce at all. We can conclude, from reading this, what Matthew actually meant in his gospel. Matthew's use of the word *porneia* (πορνεία) is meant to be understood in the secondary sense: sexual intercourse with close relatives, or just "unlawful marriages" in general.

The early Church had something to say about this topic as well. Origen wrote in AD 248: "*Just as a woman is an adulteress, even though she seem to be married to a man, while a former husband yet lives, so also the man who seems to marry her who has been divorced does not marry her, but, according to the declaration of our Savior, he commits adultery with her.*" – (Origen, Commentaries on Matthew 14:24) From this, we can clearly see that the early Chrisitans, still under persecution by the Roman Empire, did not recognize civil divorce at all, and considered those who "remarried" after divorce to be in a state of adultery.

Catholics are not permitted to divorce because, as followers of Jesus, we must follow his teachings, and Jesus

[82] Revised Standard Version Catholic Edition (RSVCE)

quite clearly forbade divorce. He only made a concession for unlawful marriages, in which case, we're talking about annulments not divorce.

Isn't an annulment just a Catholic divorce?

No. An annulment, or "declaration of nullity," is a judgement by the Church that a legal marriage (according to the Church's canon law) never existed. The two parties may have believed they were married, as did everyone who witnessed what they believed to be a lawful wedding, but there was some impediment on the wedding day that made the marriage unlawful according to the Church's canon law. Some examples of what might cause an impediment are as follows: extreme youth, impotence, prior marriage that was not declared null, a marriage of a Catholic outside the Church, marriages performed without the free will and consent of parties involved, coercive weddings, murder of a previous spouse, marriage between close relatives, extreme immaturity and/or extreme psychological defects making full consent impossible, failure to understand that mariage is a lifelong contract, refusal to consent to the procreation of children, etc.

The Catholic Church uses a process to fully investigate the circumstances of the marriage in question. When Church officials (called a "marriage tribunal") are satisfied that a marriage was not lawfully contracted according to canon law, then a "declaration of nullity" may be issued. Once the Church is satisfied that a Catholic was never actually married to begin with, said Catholic is then free to marry another. The Church does not always issue such annulments. Each application is measured on a case-by-case basis, and sometimes annulments are denied.

It should be pointed out here that Catholics can separate from their spouses in emergencies, or if doing so is necessary for the safety or wellbeing of the spouses and/or children. There is no sin in such necessary separation (which may require a civil divorce in some cases). So long as there is no attempt to contract another marriage, there is no need to pursue an annulment.

Hermas wrote the following in AD 80: "*What then shall the husband do, if the wife continues in this disposition* [adultery]*? Let him divorce her, and let the husband remain single. But if he divorce his wife and marries another, he too commits adultery.*" – (Hermas, The Shepherd IV:1:6) Here, we see this custom in the early Church spelled out clearly. Divorce (or "civil separation" as far as the Church is concerned) is permitted in some cases, for the safety or wellbeing of the spouse and/or children. However, "remarriage" is not possible, unless it can be determined by the Church that a lawful marriage (according to the Church's canon law) never really existed in the first place.

Why do Catholics and Protestants number the Ten Commandments differently?

If you look in the Bible, where the Ten Commandments are listed,[83] you'll immediately notice something. They're not numbered. We are told there are ten commandments, and only ten, but we immediately see there

[83] Exodus 20:2-17 and Deuteronomy 5:6-21

are about thirteen specific instructions from God. In other words, the Bible gives us thirteen specific instructions, then tells us there are only ten commandments, without numbering them for us.

As a result, the numbering of these thirteen instructions, into ten commandments, has been the product of tradition found outside the Bible. The Jews had their method. The Christians had a similar one with slight differences. Later, the Christian method split into two different methods following the Protestant Reformation in the sixteenth century. The Catholics retained the older Christian method, which was similar (but not totally identical) to the Jewish method. The Protestants developed their own method which is unique.

Most notable is the Protestant emphasis on the prohibition against graven images, which the Protestants have separated out as a unique commandment by itself. In the Jewish tradition, this instruction is combined together with the instruction to only worship God. In the Catholic (older Christian) tradition, this is all part of the First Commandment: "Only worship God, don't worship false gods and don't make idols of them."

Because the numbering of the commandments is an extra-Biblical tradition, not found in the Bible, there really is no right or wrong way to do it, so long as you end up with ten. The Catholic (older Christian) method puts an emphasis on the context of God being the only object of worship, in the first few instructions, keeping them lumped together into one commandment. This is closer to the Jewish method. The Protestant method seems to place an inordinate emphasis on the instruction against graven images. This may be due to the iconoclastic influences of Islam lingering in Europe after the Crusades and Reconquista, and/or the result of friction between Protestants and the Catholic Church.

Why do Catholics use the rosary when the Bible says not to pray in "vain repetitions?"

First of all, Catholics are not required to pray the rosary. It's considered a "private devotion," but it is nevertheless an extremely popular one among Catholics (even among some Anglicans), and since the Middle Ages, it has been used as a substitute of the Divine Office (Liturgy of the Hours) among lay Christians. Many stories of healing, conversion and answered prayer are attributed to regular recitation of the Holy Rosary.

The one and only Scripture passage often used to support the idea that God forbids repetitious prayer is in Matthew 6:7 and comes specifically from some older English translations of the Bible. "*But when ye pray, use not vain repetitions, as the heathen do: for they think that they shall be heard for their much speaking.*" – (Matthew 6:7)[84] Very few English translations use the phrase "*vain repetitions.*" Most instead translate it as "babbling" or "babbling on," and this is probably a reference to the events recorded in 1st Kings 18:25-29 when the Pagan priests of Baal called upon their idol for hours while cutting themselves.

[84] King James Version, AD 1611

The problem here appears to be the Greek word *battalogeo* (βατταλογέω) which some older English versions[85] translate as "vain repetitions." The word itself is a contraction of two Greek words: *batta* and *logeo.* Literally translated, *batta* means "babbling" and *logeo* means "words" or "many words." So transliterated the phrase in question reads: "*use not babbling words.*"[86] For some unknown reason, the older English translators, in England and Switzerland, decided to put more emphasis on the plurality of "words" in *logeo*, and less emphasis on "babbling" in *batta.* Thus, instead of translating *battalogeo* as "babbling words" or "babbling on and on," they came up with "vain repetitions." Go figure! Needless to say, this is no longer the case with most English translations. The problem seems to have begun with the Geneva Bible (1599), which was outspokenly anti-Catholic. The King James Version (1611) then followed suit and the rest is history. Regardless of the political rationale behind it, this way of translating the verse is just plain wrong. Even the Wycliffe Bible (1395), which is an English translation that predates both the King James and Geneva versions by more than two centuries, doesn't translate the verse this way. It simply reads: "*But in praying do not ye speak much, as heathen men do, for they guess that they be heard in their much speech.*"[87]

Clearly, Jesus did not give a blanket condemnation of repeating a meaningful prayer. On the contrary, the original Greek tells us that what he forbade was the senseless babbling that some people once did in a vain attempt to get

[85] Older English Versions: particularly the King James Version (1611) and the Geneva Bible (1599).

[86] Transliteration directly from Greek into English

[87] Matthew 6:7, Wycliffe Bible (1395)

their idol's attention. As in all things we should look to the example of Jesus to understand his intent. Jesus himself repeated his prayer to God the Father in Matthew 26:44, and he praised the tax collector who repeated his prayer multiple times in Luke 18:13. St Paul told the Thessalonians to pray without ceasing in 1st Thessalonians 5:17 and the Book of Revelation tells us that God is surrounded by creatures who pray the same thing over and over again.[88] There is nothing in the Bible that forbids repetitive prayers, so long as they are meaningful. In fact, the Bible actually published them (Psalm 136). What is forbidden is senseless babbling that doesn't make sense, so as to try to get God's attention, as if he somehow has difficulty hearing us.

Is the pope the Antichrist?

While this question may seem ridiculous to many people, you might be surprised to discover just how many Evangelicals actually believe it, or are at least suspicious of it. The notion comes from the first Protestant reformer himself – Martin Luther[89] – in the sixteenth century, who asserted that the ***office*** of the papacy is the Antichrist. That's not to say any particular pope, but the office of the papacy itself.[90] So when German Protestantism began to mix with

---

[88] Revelation 4:8

[89] Martin Luther – the sixteenth century German Protestant reformer, not to be confused with Martin Luther King, the twentieth century American civil rights activist.

[90] While most Lutherans today have dropped this teaching, some have not. In particular, as of the date of this writing, the Missouri Synod Lutheran Church (LCMS), as well as the Wisconsin Synod Lutheran

Protestantism in the United Kingdom and the United States during the nineteenth century, you can imagine what an explosive combination this created. As new UK and US Protestant denominations were formed, the office of the papacy went from being the Antichrist on a political-rhetorical level, to the actual incarnation of evil itself!

This notion has become very popular among some Evangelicals in the United States today, and is a bit humorous when you really stop and think about it. Before we start levelling the accusation of "Antichrist" at anybody, or any office, it might help to actually understand what the Bible has to say about it. After all, the whole idea of "Antichrist" is a Biblical concept.

So what does the Bible say about the Antichrist? Well, for starters, the Bible tells us that the "spirit of antichrist" was alive and well even during the Apostolic age. [91] It also tells us that in order to be antichrist in any way, one must deny that Jesus of Nazareth is the promised Jewish Messiah.[92] One must also deny that God the Son came to earth in the form of flesh and blood.[93] These are the only four times the word "antichrist" appears in the Scriptures. So based on the Biblical definition, to be an antichrist (or even THE Antichrist) one must deny that Jesus of Nazareth is the promised Messiah ***and*** one must deny that God the

Church (WELS), still officially teach that the "office" of the papacy (not the pope himself) is the Antichrist.

[91] 1st John 2:18

[92] 1st John 2:22

[93] 1st John 4:3; 2nd John 1:7

Son came to earth in the form of human flesh. Sorry, that's just the Biblical definition, and since the term "Antichrist" is a Biblical term, just like the term "Christ" itself, it has no real meaning outside this Biblical definition.

Now since every pope since the time of St Peter has affirmed that Jesus of Nazareth is the Messianic Son of God, that sort of disqualifies every pope in history from being an antichrist. Of course, the office of the papacy itself was founded on St Peter's affirmation that Jesus of Nazareth is the promised Messianic Son of God,[94] so that disqualifies the papal office from being antichrist. Since the pope literally teaches, and his office is literally founded upon, the belief that Jesus of Nazareth is the Messianic Son of God, it is literally impossible (in every Biblical sense) for the pope, or his papal office, to be the Antichrist in any way. Again, sorry if this bursts your bubble, but Scripture speaks for itself here. To assert that the pope, or the papacy, is somehow, in any way, the Antichrist, is to completely deny the plain and clear teaching of the Bible on this matter. Now, if some people want to go ahead and call the pope the Antichrist anyway, then they can go ahead, but in doing so, the rest of us need to understand they are directly contradicting the Bible when they do this.

Wasn't Constantine the first pope?

No. St Peter was the first pope, and this is attested by all the writings of antiquity. Nobody in ancient times, not even Christianity's fiercest critics, doubted that. The early Christians were obsessed with lines of apostolic succession,

[94] Matthew 16:15-19

as a way of tracing who had authentic authority from the Apostles and who did not. This is so well documented in antiquity, that anyone who says otherwise just can't be taken seriously. To deny such well-documented history is to deny history itself. I've included the complete list of *pontificates* (papal administrations) in the first appendix section at the end of this book.

The "Constantine Conspiracy" was invented sometime in the last 200 years and most likely originated in Scotland.[95] Since then, this cabal has been promulgated by Protestant Fundamentalists of various types and the Jehovah's Witnesses. It relies heavily on the historical ignorance of most Christians in order to be accepted. In other words, in order to believe this whopper of a tale, you've got to be completely ignorant of ancient Church history.

Constantine (the Great) was not a pope. He wasn't even a Christian until he was baptized on his deathbed. Rather, he was an emperor of the Roman Empire. His reign lasted from AD 306 to 337. The six popes who reigned during this time were: St Marcellus I (AD 308-309), St Eusebius (AD 309-310), St Miltiades (AD 311-314), St Sylvester I (AD 314-335), St Mark (AD 336), and St Julius I (AD 337-352). Again, see the list of pontificates at the end of this book in Appendix 1.

[95] Most "Constantine conspiracists" trace their citations back to the works of Alexander Hislop (AD 1807-1865), a minister in the Free Church of Scotland, whose works have been debunked by reputable historians.

Constantine is famous for four major acts that changed the course of Church history in the ancient world. While Constantine was not a Christian, his mother (Helena) was. This likely explains his initial sympathy for Christianity, which later developed into curiosity, interest and finally conversion.

Once he assumed absolute power as the Emperor of Rome, one of his first major acts was the Edict of Milan in AD 313, also known as the "Edict of Toleration," which legalized Christianity as a legitimate religion within the Roman Empire (equal with all other religions of the empire), and made it illegal to persecute Christians for their faith. It also provided for some reparations to be made to the churches for their previous troubles.

The second major thing he did was call for Christians to resolve their own doctrinal disputes concerning the Arian Heresy. This is what gave rise to the Council of Nicea in AD 325, which put down Arius and his followers, established the Nicene Creed, and called for the creation of a universal New Testament that would be used by all Christians everywhere. It should be noted here that other than calling for the council, Constantine had no administrative role within the council. That was an internal Church matter between the pope and bishops.

Third, as a result of the Nicene Council, he enforced a break between the Hebrew calendar and the calculated date for Easter, making sure Christians would henceforth use the Julian calendar for the celebration of Easter, and all movable feasts within Christianity, in accordance with the decision of the Nicene fathers.

Fourth and finally, he split the Roman Empire in two, East and West, and established its new capital in Byzantium (in Asia Minor), which he renamed after himself – Constantinople.[96] The decision to split the empire was mainly administrative in nature, but in Constantinople, Christianity found greater opportunities to gain a foothold in government affairs, garnering greater protection and support from the empire itself.

That was Constantine's civil contributions to the Christian Faith, acting as a civil ruler, not as a pope. No credible historian would ever call Constantine a "pope." That is the stuff of anti-Catholic, conspiracy theories.

There was a Pope Constantine in the early eighth-century, perhaps this is where some of the confusion arises for regular Christians approached by anti-Catholic conspiricists. However, this is not the same Constantine who was emperor of Rome in the early fourth-century. In the case of this later Pope Constantine (AD 708-715), he was simply named after the Roman emperor who reigned four centuries prior (AD 306-337).

Didn't Constantine invent the Catholic Church and introduce Pagan beliefs into Christianity at that time?

No. This is part of the "Constantine Conspiracy" described above. Again, the conspiracy theory most likely derives from Scotland, less than two centuries ago, among anti-Catholic Protestant ministers. It has since been

[96] Constantinople: today known as Istanbul in modern Turkey.

promulgated around the globe by Protestant Fundamentalists of various types and the Jehovah's Witnesses. The conspiracy theory relies on the notion that the teachings and practices of Roman Catholicism did not exist within Christianity prior to AD 313, when Emperor Constantine issued the Edict of Milan, ending the persecution of Christianity in the Roman Empire.

In order for the conspiracy to be believable, there can be no evidence of Catholic doctrines, traditions, or practices within Christianity prior to the reign of Emperor Constantine (AD 306-337). The only problem is, as I stated earlier in this book, the early Christians were prolific writers, and antiquity is littered with evidence that clearly demonstrates Catholic beliefs, traditions and practices in the early Church, dating back decades, or even centuries, before Emperor Constatine. Some of that evidence is cited in this book.

Isn't the Catholic Church the "Whore of Babylon" from the Book of Revelation?

No. The early Christians referred to the ancient City of Rome as "Babylon,"[97] but this was in reference to the Caesar worship of the ancient Roman Empire. The term "Babylon" recalls the Jewish experience in literal Babylon during their captivity centuries prior (605-537 BC), wherein they were commanded to worship the Babylonian king as a god.[98]

[97] St Peter referred to ancient Rome as "Babylon" in 1st Peter 5:13
[98] Daniel 3

The early Christians considered the Church in Rome a completely different entity that had nothing to do with Pagan Rome (Babylon) itself. In St John's *Book of Revelation*,[99] the phrase "Mystery Babylon" was used to describe a city that metaphorically "prostituted itself" (a biblical reference to an unholy alliance) with the worship of kings. The Biblical phrase "Whore of Babylon" is associated with the ancient Pagan City of Rome, which so freely gave itself over to emperor worship. The once proud city, with its republican form of government, and freedom of religion, had gone the way of so many imperial capitals before it, worshipping their king as a god, demanding that everyone (regardless of religion or cult) give him homage.

The term "Whore of Babylon" has nothing to do with the ancient Church within Rome, and nothing to do with the Roman Catholic Church that emerged from it in the centuries that followed. The "Whore of Babylon" (Pagan Rome), with its mandatory cult of Caesar worship, eventually ceased to be, only to later be sacked by Germanic hordes and left in ruins.

The hill upon which the modern Vatican[100] stands, *Mons Vaticanus*, existed outside the city limits of ancient Rome, across the Tiber River, and was not part of the old city.[101] During the middle to late first-century, when the *Book of Revelation* was written, *Mons Vaticanus* was the dusty

[99] Revelation 17

[100] Vatican: the pope's primary residence and modern headquarters of the Roman Catholic Church

[101] The ancient city of Rome was built on seven hills called "mountains" or *mons*, named as follows: Aventine, Caelian, Capitoline, Esquiline, Palatine, Quirinal and Viminal.

elevation outside the city, used for chariot racing. Later, during the reign of Nero Caesar, a circus was built there which was frequently used to execute Christians. It is believed that St Peter was crucified upside-down at the *Circus Vaticanus* built on *Mons Vaticanus*. Nearby was a catacomb of tombs where many Christians were buried, including St Peter. The modern St Peter's Basilica (the largest church in today's Vatican-City complex) was built directly over the tomb of St Peter, and covers these catacombs. All of this was outside the City of Rome when the *Book of Revelation* was written. The author of *Revelation*, St John, specifically mentions the seven hills upon which the mystery city (Babylon) is built.[102] *Mons Vaticanus* is not included in that list. Once again, just to be clear, *Mons Vaticanus* (where the Vatican City-State now stands), was not part of ancient Rome. It was outside the city and across the river. St John would be aghast that anyone would connect his "Mystery Babylon" reference in *Revelation* with the Catholic Church, or any Christian entity for that matter.

Connecting the Catholic Church to the "Whore of Babylon" is part of the "Constantine Conspiracy," as described above. It would appear that nineteenth-century Protestant ministers in Scotland pulled heavily from Martin Luther's work in sixteenth-century Germany.[103] Luther used academic rhetoric to assert that the papacy was leading Christians into a type of "Babylonain Captivity" with its teachings about the seven sacraments. The phrase pulls from Biblical illustration, citing the captivity of the Jews in

---

[102] Revelation 17:9

[103] Martin Luther, *On the Babylonian Captivity of the Church*, AD 1520

Babylon from 605 BC to 537 BC. In typical Luther fashion, he drew parallels between Biblical events and current events in his time, as he perceived them. It's not uncommon for Christian writers to do this, but the object of Luther's attack was clearly Rome, the Vatican and the papacy itself. He compared modern Rome to Babylon, not literally but rhetorically.

There was a tendency in nineteenth-century Protestant Scotland to take the writings of Martin Luther to a literal extreme, far more so than most German Lutherans ever did. What Luther said about modern Rome in a rhetorical sense, Scottish ministers took in a literal sense. Not just the modern City of Rome, but the Roman Catholic Church itself, became to them "Mystery Babylon" or the "Whore of Babylon" from the *Book of Revelation.*

This radical interpretation was exported around the world, especially to the United States, where it took root among Protestant Fundamentalists and the Jehovah's Witnesses in the late nineteenth to early twentieth centuries. While fading fast, and not nearly as prolific as it once was, this radical interpretation of Luther's writings still finds itself circulating among some Evangelicals today.

Doesn't God hate religion, and isn't Christianity really about having a personal relationship with God?

If God hates religion he certainly has a funny way of showing it, since he actually invented the most complex and demanding religion in the world – ancient Judaism. In recent decades, it has become in vogue for some Evangelicals to insist that God is opposed to religion in general, and prefers people to instead have a personal relationship with him. While it is certainly true that God wants us to have a personal relationship with him, and that popes have spoken extensively on this very thing,[104] it is also true that God never intended such a personal relationship to be private.

There is a difference you see, between personal and private. This personal relationship we are supposed to have with God is simultaneously supposed to be a public one. God made his new covenant with a community not individuals. Individuals can share in that covenant by being initiated into the community God has covenanted with. Religion (true Christian religion that is) is simply the way people organize their personal relationship with God into a public and communal expression that is both orderly and dignified.[105] Thus, religion and relationship complement each other. They are not opposed to one another.

In the case of Catholicism, that religion was organized by the Apostles of Jesus Christ and their successors (the popes and bishops). There is nothing in the Scriptures that condemns religion in and of itself. However, there are plenty of Scripture passages that condemn the hypocritical abuse of religion for personal gain. So no, God does not hate religion, and yes, Christianity is about having a personal relationship with Jesus Christ. That personal

[104] Pope John Paul II, speech to bishops of Southern Germany, December 4, 1992; Pope Benedict XVI, Angelus, Vatican City, February 26, 2012

[105] Catechism of the Catholic Church, paragraphs 1140 & 2105

relationship is public, not private, and Christian religion helps us express it publicly and in community.

CHAPTER 3: THE BIBLE

Do Catholics believe in the Bible?

Yes! In fact, Catholics invented the Bible. Shocking as that may sound, it is historically accurate to say that. The New Testament did not exist as a single compilation prior to AD 367. Before then, most of the writings of the New Testament were on parchment scrolls and scattered throughout the churches of the ancient Roman Empire. They were mixed together with other writings that were orthodox but not necessarily inspired Scripture. No two regions of the early Church had the exact same scrolls, nor the exact same *number* of scrolls. It was all rather chaotic.

In response to the Arian heresy in the early fourth century, the Catholic Church commissioned its bishops to find out which scrolls should belong to a universal New Testament that all Christians would use. Many committees were held to determine this based on Catholic Tradition.

In AD 367, a Catholic bishop in Northern Africa, St Athanasius of Alexandria, approved (for his diocese) a particular set of twenty-seven scrolls, consisting of the writings of Matthew through Revelation. Three Catholic councils[106] were then held to ratify this list, and in AD 405, these twenty-seven scrolls were declared to be the universal New Testament by Pope Innocent I. This is the same New Testament we all use today, Catholics and Protestants alike,

[106] Councils of Rome (AD 382), Hippo (AD 393) and Carthage (AD 397)

including Evangelicals, thanks to the hard and faithful work of the Catholic Church sixteen hundred years ago.[107]

Do Catholics read the Bible?

Yes, we actually do, perhaps even more so than some Evangelicals, if you can believe that. This is because some of us not only read the Bible on our own, but we have the Bible read to us at Mass every day of the week. In fact, if a Catholic simply attends Mass every Sunday, he will have heard nearly the entire Bible read to him over the course of three years. If he attends Mass every day, which a small few do, he will have heard nearly the whole Bible read to him three times in four years. This doesn't even include the liturgy itself, which is chalk full of Scripture passages from the Bible. Just attending Mass is like going to a Bible-fest! The priest reads the Bible. The people respond with memorized responses heavily based on Bible verses.

Then, if the Catholic prays the Divine Office (Liturgy of the Hours), he again is exposed to an extremely hefty portion of Scripture. Some Catholics attend Bible studies on top of that, and some read and study the Bible on their own. In fact, the Catholic Church actively exhorts Catholics to read and study the Bible.[108] What Catholics do not generally do is memorize Biblical passages in rote, with the chapter and verse numbers attached. This is a common Evangelical practice not usually shared by Catholics. So if one is expecting to hear a Catholic rattle off a Bible verse

[107] Catechism of the Catholic Church, paragraph 120

[108] Catechism of the Catholic Church, paragraphs 104, 131 & 133

with a chapter and verse attached, one will likely be disappointed. Thus, it might superficially appear that the Catholic is Biblically illiterate, though that's not the case at all. Now if a Catholic doesn't attend Mass, then he's not a good Catholic, and of course by not attending Mass, he's probably not reading or hearing much of the Bible either. The same can sometimes be true of Evangelicals; however, Evangelicals have been known to study the Bible on their own, without regular church attendance.

Why do Catholic Bibles have more books than Protestant Bibles?

The short answer is to say that Catholics kept the books that Protestants removed from the Bible. Now here is the long answer.

You see, the canon of the Bible was basically settled in AD 405. However, over a thousand years later, the German Reformer, Martin Luther, decided to move seven books from the Old Testament (Tobit, Judith, 1st Maccabees, 2nd Maccabees, Wisdom, Sirach and Baruch) into a separate section he called *apocrypha* (meaning "disputed"). Luther then moved portions of the Old Testament books of Esther and Daniel into this *apocrypha* section as well. Now in Luther's defense, we could say that he was only following the standardized Jewish canon being used in Europe at that time. However, what many people don't know is that the standardized scriptural canon, used in mediaeval Jewish synagogues, developed as the result of mainstream Judaism coming under the control of the Pharisee Party after the fall of the Jerusalem Temple in AD

70. The Pharisees had their own list of canonical books, which was shorter than the Old Testament canonical books used by the Apostles, and most Jewish communities in the Mediterranean world.

The Apostles used the more popular Greek translation of the Jewish canon (*Septuagint*) which contained more books than the Pharisaical Jewish canon (*Tanakh*). This Greek Jewish Bible (*Septuagint*) was the canon of Scripture used by the majority of Jews outside of Palestine in the first century. So this is the one the Apostles preferred, and quoted from, frequently in their own writings (gospels and epistles). As the good news of Jesus Christ spread throughout the ancient world, Jews came under tremendous pressure to choose between the Christians and the Pharisees. Those Jews who sided with the Christians just became known as "Christians" along with the rest, and were eventually "put out of the synagogue" (excommunicated from Judaism). The Jews, who sided with the Pharisees against Christianity, then adopted many Pharisaical practices, which included: the rejection of Christian claims of Jesus as the promised Messiah, the use of the shorter Pharisaical canon (*Tanakh*), the mandatory reading of that canon in Hebrew (as opposed to Greek), and a host of other standardizations. Thus, the new standardized Jewish canon (*Tanakh*) came to be shorter than the Christian Old Testament canon (*Septuagint*).[109]

[109] Except in Ethiopia. Ethiopian Jews did not come under the influence of the Pharisees after the fall of the Temple in AD 70. So they still use the Greek-translated *Septuagint*.

So the real question in play here is this. Who had the authority to determine the Christian Old Testament canon? Did that authority belong to the Apostles and early Church? Or did it belong to the first-century Pharisee Party that rejected Jesus Christ and the claims of the early Church?

Luther may have had his own reasons for moving some Old Testament books out of the official canon and into his "apocrypha" section, but the premise of this decision is identical to that of the late, first-century Pharisees. He based it on an authority that was non-Apostolic. He based his shorter (39-book) Old Testament on the claims of a Jewish authority that rejected Jesus Christ and his Apostles. Today, Protestant scholars go to great lengths to explain why some of these books should be excluded from the Christian Old Testament canon, but again, they base this on academics, not actual Apostolic authority. The fact is, the Apostles primarily used, and quoted from, the longer (46-book) *Septuagint.* The early Church regarded this as equally authoritative and on par with the Hebrew *Tanakh* used by the Pharisees. If the longer (46-book) Old Testament (*Septuagint*) was good enough for the Apostles and the early Church, why should it not be good enough for us today?

What many people don't know is that Martin Luther also tried to remove four books from the New Testament as well (Hebrews, James, Jude and Revelation). His rationale was that these books didn't carry the same weight as the rest of the New Testament, based entirely on his own academic judgement. In other words, they didn't agree with his theology. So he wanted to downgrade them to "less than Scripture," or *apocrypha* (disputed).

Martin Luther is considered the father of the Protestant Reformation, and all Protestants (including Evangelicals) rely on his judgement about the canon of the Bible. His removal of seven Old Testament books from the regular canon, along with his shortening of Esther and Daniel, became a very popular trend among Protestants throughout sixteenth-century Europe[110] and remains so to this day. However, his attempted removal of the four New Testament books was ultimately rejected by all, and eventually forgotten to history.

The Catholic Church however, does not believe that any modern scholar, priest or bishop, (not even the pope himself) has the authority to alter the Biblical text, regardless of the level of academic reasoning that goes behind it.[111] So Catholics use the longer (46-book) Old Testament originally used by the Apostles and early Christians.

It's interesting to note that most English-Protestant Bible publishers continued to print the so-called *apocrypha* books up until the late nineteenth century. Even the original version of the highly esteemed King James Bible retained

[110] Thirty-Nine Articles of Religion (Anglicanism AD 1563); Westminster Confession of Faith (Calvinism AD 1647); from these two confessions come the thirty-nine-book Old Testament in the English-speaking Protestant world.

[111] *De Canonicis Scripturis*, Council of Trent (AD 1546); Session 11, Council of Florence (AD 1442); Synod of Rome (AD 382); Synod of Hippo (AD 393); Synod of Carthage (AD 397); Decree of Pope Innocent I (AD 405)

the so-called *apocrypha* books, and continued to print them until the 1880's. The complete absence of the so-called *apocrypha* books from virtually all English-Protestant Bibles is a relatively modern phenomenon unique to the twentieth and twenty-first centuries. In recent decades, however, it has become in vogue for some Bible publishers to print Bibles that include all of the books they previously removed. So, just a century after completely removing those books from their printed Bibles, some Protestant publishers are starting to put them back in. Is your Bible complete? Or are you using a truncated version? Check your Old Testament to see if it contains the following books: Tobit, Judith, 1st Maccabees, 2nd Maccabees, Wisdom, Sirach and Baruch. If it doesn't, you have a truncated Old Testament that is missing books regarded as Scripture by the Apostles, thanks to the intervention of Martin Luther and the Protestant Reformers. Perhaps it's time to consider getting a Bible with a complete Old Testament. A complete list of canonical books, both Old Testament and New, is included in the second appendix at the end of this book.

Do Catholics follow the Bible alone?

No. Catholics do not follow the Bible **alone** because it's not Biblical to do that. The idea of following the Bible **alone** comes from the German father of the Protestant Reformation, Martin Luther, who in AD 1520 declared *Sola Scriptura* as one of his five *solas*, or pillars, of German Protestantism. The Latin phrase *Sola Scriptura* means "Scripture Only," commonly referred to as the "Bible Alone." There is no Biblical passage that can back this idea. In fact, the Bible suggests the exact opposite. The canon of

Scripture itself, which is the list of books that make up the Bible, is not anywhere recorded in the actual text of Scripture. So if we go by the concept of the "Bible Alone," we don't really know what books should belong in the Bible to begin with.

The Bible also tells us specifically to **follow the traditions** of the Church,[112] whether written in the Scriptures, or given orally.[113] It tells us to shun those who do not keep the **traditions** of the Church[114] and tells us that Scripture should never even be interpreted independently of the Church.[115] Jesus himself commanded his own Apostles to follow the traditions of the Jewish leaders[116] because they held the authority of succession from Moses. What Jesus condemned was not tradition in and of itself, but rather the hypocrisy of the Jewish leaders of his time, who abused tradition for their own financial and political gain.[117] This is a common misunderstanding on the part of many (not all but many) Evangelicals. They mistake Jesus' condemnation of hypocrisy for a blanket condemnation of tradition in general.

No, Catholics do not follow the Bible alone, because the Bible basically tells us not to. Catholics instead follow both Sacred Scripture (the Bible) and Apostolic Tradition,

[112] 1st Corinthians 11:1
[113] 2nd Thessalonians 2:15
[114] 2nd Thessalonians 3:6
[115] 2nd Peter 1:20; 2nd Peter 3:15-16
[116] Matthew 23:2-3
[117] Matthew 15:1-8

which is conveyed to us through the teaching authority of the Catholic Church.

Wait! Doesn't the Bible tell us to follow the Bible alone?

No, it does not. As I said above, there is not a single Biblical passage that instructs Christians to follow the Bible **alone**. That being the case, no Christian can be held to Martin Luther's rule of *Sola Scriptura.* Perhaps some Christians may voluntarily submit to it, but no Christian can be forced to follow it, because it's not in the Bible. One common objection, used by some Evangelicals, is found in the second epistle of St Paul to Timothy: *"All scripture, inspired of God, is profitable to teach, to reprove, to correct, to instruct in justice, That the man of God may be perfect, furnished to every good work."* – (2nd Timothy 3:16-17) However, it should be pointed out here that the passage specifically says "***All*** *Scripture*" not "***Only*** *Scripture.*" So it can in no way be used as a prooftext for *Sola Scriptura.* Another common objection is found in St Paul's first epistle to the Church in Corinth: *"I have applied all this to myself and Apollos for your benefit, brethren, that you may learn by us* ***not to go beyond what is written****, that none of you may be puffed up in favor of one against another."* – (1st Corinthians 4:6)[118] This is how the passage is commonly translated into most modern English versions of the Bible, and because of this, it is commonly used as a prooftext for *Sola Scriptura* by some Evangelicals.

[118] Revised Standard Version Catholic Edition (RSVCE), emphasis mine

However, this is one example where I think the older English versions do a much better job picking up on the nuance of ancient Jewish idioms. Here we have the same verse from the 1610 Douay-Rheims Bible: *"But these things, brethren, I have in a figure transferred to myself and to Apollo, for your sakes; that in us you may learn, that one be* ***not puffed up against the other for another, above that which is written****."* – (1st Corinthians 4:6)[119] Then of course the much esteemed 1611 King James Bible so eloquently puts the same verse this way: *"And these things, brethren, I have in a figure transferred to myself and to Apollos for your sakes; that ye might learn in us* ***not to think of men above that which is written****, that no one of you be puffed up for one against another."* – (1st Corinthians 4:6)[120] As you can see, once the nuance of this Jewish idiom is interpreted, it radically clarifies the inferred meaning of the passage. It's also contextual, you see, because in this chapter, St Paul is telling the Corinthians not to be divided in their leadership. Nowhere in this chapter does St Paul discuss the canon of Scripture, or why Christians should only believe in the Scriptures **alone**.

Then of course, there is the all too common objection from the Book of Revelation that pronounces a curse upon anyone who adds to the Scriptures: "*For I testify to every one that heareth the words of the prophecy of this book: If any man shall add to these things, God shall add unto him the plagues written in this book.*" – (Revelation 22:18) However, this is a curse upon anyone who adds to the Book of Revelation in particular, and it is followed by a curse upon anyone who

[119] Emphasis mine

[120] King James Version, emphasis mine

removes portions of the Book of Revelation: "*And if any man shall take away from the words of the book of this prophecy, God shall take away his part out of the book of life, and out of the holy city, and from these things that are written in this book.*" – (Revelation 22:19) These two curses pertain specifically to the Book of Revelation and have nothing to do with extra-Biblical traditions. To say otherwise does gross violence to the context of the passage.

Even if we play devil's advocate, and presume this passage does apply to the whole Bible, we have to limit it to adding or removing Scripture. (There's still nothing here about traditions.) So if that's the case, the curse applies to the Protestant Reformers, not the Catholic Church, for the Catholic Church has faithfully fought to retain all the books of the Biblical canon, while the Protestant Reformers fought to remove some of them. Thankfully, for the Protestant Reformers, this passage only applies to the Book of Revelation, which they wisely left untouched, except for Martin Luther. He tried to remove the whole Book of Revelation from the New Testament canon entirely.

In all fairness to Martin Luther, what is now commonly understood as *Sola Scriptura,* in most Evangelical communities, is not what he actually meant when he coined the phrase. The original definition of *Sola Scriptura*, from a Lutheran perspective, is that Scripture is the **only infallible** source of divine revelation. Therefore, all other things, including Christian traditions, must be subject to the infallible teaching of Scripture alone, but that doesn't mean they should automatically be rejected just because they're not explicitly found in the Bible.

From a Catholic perspective, there are problems with this understanding too. As the canon of Scripture itself was created by the infallible proclamations of the Church, not the Bible. Therefore, logic would dictate that sources of infallibility can likewise be found outside of the Bible, both in Apostolic Tradition and the occasional proclamations of the Church. The Bible points to the Church (not itself) as "*the pillar and bulwark of the truth.*" – (1st Timothy 3:15)[121]

This, however, is an argument for Catholic and Lutheran theologians to hammer out in the course of ecumenical discussions. What *Sola Scriptura* has effectively become, in the emerging Evangelical mainstream, might even be considered heretical from a Lutheran point of view. Namely the notion that if a doctrine is not explicitly (or at least implicitly) found in the Bible; it is to be rejected. As far as I know, this was never Luther's intent when he coined the term.

Unfortunately, this very anti-Biblical notion is becoming more and more popular in the emerging Evangelical mainstream. It is both unreasonable, and unbiblical, for Christians to insist that every article of faith and practice **must** be found in the Bible. It's also self-contradicting. Evangelicals would do well to go back to Martin Luther's original intent for *Sola Scriptura* and acknowledge at least the possibility of legitimate extra-Biblical beliefs and practices. Then we can reasonably discuss the authority for such things. To just dismiss them out of hand, however, simply because they're not explicitly

[121] Revised Standard Version Catholic Edition (RSVCE)

(or at least implicitly) found in the Bible, is a very unbiblical thing to do.

Didn't the medieval Catholic Church chain Bibles to altars, burn vernacular Bible translations and intentionally try to prevent the people from reading the Scriptures by keeping them in Latin?

The Catholic Church has ***never*** tried to keep the Scriptures away from the people. In fact, the Catholic Church was the first to commission vernacular translations of the Bible. The Latin Bible (*Vulgate*) itself was a vernacular translation from the original Greek and Hebrew text. As for vernacular translations into modern languages, many within the Catholic Church actually worked very hard to make this happen. Let's take the English language for example. In the late seventh century, a large compilation of the Bible was translated into Old English by St Bede. Later, Richard Rolle made a significant update as the English language changed, translating the Biblical Psalter into Middle English in the early fourteenth century. All of these were done by Catholics for Catholic England long before the English Reformation. To say the Catholic Church was negligent in translating the Scriptures into modern vernaculars is patently untrue. The only time in history when the Church permitted Bibles to be burned was when it was determined that the particular translation in question was flawed and presented heresy. In such cases, properly translated Bibles were offered to replace them.

As for chaining Bibles to altars, that did happen a very long time ago, but not to keep the Bible away from the people. On the contrary, it was to make sure Bibles were ***not*** taken away from the people. You see, back during the Middle Ages, before the age of the printing press, Bibles were copied by hand. Thus, they were extremely expensive. One Bible could easily cost an entire year's salary for an average working man. The problem was that with such an expensive book sitting on the altar, it would be very easy for it to be stolen, taken to another city, and sold at a very handsome profit. So to prevent this from happening, and to make sure the people of the parish retained access to the Sacred Scriptures, these expensive Bibles were chained to the altars for safe keeping. This way, any common parishioner (assuming he was literate) could easily go to the church on any day, walk up to the altar, and always have a Bible available to read to his heart's content.

Now, the false assertion that the Catholic Church was trying to keep the Scriptures away from the people in the Middle Ages is often made with the false assumption that the Catholic Church was trying to hide the gospel from the people. This again is patently false, and a bit ridiculous when you stop and think about it. The whole mission of the Catholic Church has always been to convey the message of the gospel, and in the vastly illiterate world of the Middle Ages, the Church did this by using all means at its disposal. Of course, clergy were trained to read the Scriptures, and convey them to the people in their regular homilies (sermons). Likewise poems and songs, which could be easily memorized, were employed for this purpose too. In addition, the Church hired artists to paint and carve images, which could likewise be used as teaching tools to educate the populace. We use this exact same pictorial method in illustrated children's books today. The Catholic Church did a remarkable job conveying the gospel to a world without literacy, the printing press, television, radio or the Internet.

CHAPTER 4: MARY AND THE SAINTS

Do Catholics worship Mary?

No, Catholics do not worship Mary,[122] nor do we worship anyone, nor anything, other than the Trinitarian God: Father, Son and Holy Spirit. The Catholic Church condemns the worship of anyone or anything else as idolatry [123] and such idolatry could be punishable by excommunication, if such an idolator does not repent.

If Catholics don't worship Mary, why do they pray to her?

Catholics pray to Mary, other Saints and the holy angels, because we do not believe prayer, in and of itself, is worship. Catholics understand worship in the Biblical sense, which usually involves the presentation of an actual flesh and blood sacrifice.[124] This, coupled with the act of adoration (full submission of the mind, body, soul and will) is how Catholics understand worship in the usual Biblical sense. In the act of Holy Communion we unite ourselves with Christ's perfect sacrifice, thus participating in real

[122] Worship: meaning *adoration*, to acknowledge as God, and give full act of submission to divinity

[123] Catechism of the Catholic Church, paragraphs 2112 - 2114

[124] Genesis 4:4; Genesis 8:20; Exodus 22:20; 1st Samuel 15:22; Romans 5:10; 1st Corinthians 5:7; 1st Peter 2:5

Biblical worship.[125] The mere act of prayer is simply to offer requests and does not, in and of itself, constitute worship in the full Biblical sense.

Why pray to Mary and the Saints at all, when you can take your prayers directly to God?

As Catholics, we do take our prayers directly to God all the time. We do so publicly during the Divine Liturgy (Holy Mass) and also during the Divine Office (Liturgy of the Hours), as well as during the administration of all the sacraments. We also take our prayers directly to God during private devotion as well. In addition to this, we also pray to Mary, the Saints and the holy angels, because we view them as "prayer partners" in our common devotion to the same God.[126] They assist us in our prayers in the sense that they pray *with* us to God. Just as we ask friends and neighbors, in this world, to pray for us, so we also ask our friends in the next world to pray for us as well. The Bible itself gives us indications that this is a wholesome and acceptable practice.[127] Likewise, the early Church affirmed this practice among the early Christians, still persecuted for their Faith by the Romans. As Origen wrote in AD 233: "*But not the high priest* [Christ] *alone prays for those who pray sincerely, but also the angels... as also the souls of the Saints who have already fallen asleep.*" – (Origen, Prayer 11) Cyprian of Carthage also wrote the following in AD 253: "*Let us remember one another in concord and*

[125] Catechism of the Catholic Church, paragraphs 2099 - 2100

[126] Catechism of the Catholic Church, paragraphs 2683 - 2684

[127] Tobit 12:12; Mark 12:26-27; Mark 9:4; Hebrews 12:1; Revelation 5:8; Revelation 8:4

unanimity. Let us on both sides [of death] always pray for one another. Let us relieve burdens and afflictions by mutual love, that if one of us, by the swiftness of divine condescension, shall go hence first, our love may continue in the presence of the Lord, and our prayers for our brethren and sisters not cease in the presence of the Father's mercy." – (Cyprian of Carthage, Letters 56[60]:5)

How is praying to the Saints not necromancy or witchcraft which is forbidden in the Bible?

There is absolutely nothing in the Bible that forbids praying to the Saints. Jesus himself did it in Mark 9:4.[128] If it's good enough for the Son of God, then it should be good enough for us.

The Scripture passage that is commonly used here, in an attempt to equate prayer to Saints with necromancy or witchcraft, is Deuteronomy 18:10, in which God strictly forbids witchcraft. This is then combined with the Scripture that recalls King Saul's encounter with the witch at Endor.[129] Because the witch engaged in conjuring up the dead (a medium), it is mistakenly interpreted that any attempted contact with the dead is a form of witchcraft.

First of all, when we Catholics pray to a deceased person, we do not expect that person to answer us in a way we can hear, as is typically expected when one visits a

[128] While Jesus is divine and able to communicate with the dead freely, he was also a Jewish man under the Law of Moses when he did this. If he broke the Law of Moses he could not be God nor a perfect sacrifice for our sins. Thus simple communication with the dead, through the Holy Spirit, cannot be a violation of God's law.

[129] 1st Samuel 28

medium. Second, when we pray to a deceased person, we do so through the Holy Spirit, and it is the Holy Spirit who makes that communication possible. We make no attempt to circumvent (get around) God and talk to the dead ourselves, expecting some kind of reply apart from God. That really would be witchcraft and necromancy. The very definition of witchcraft is to attempt to do spiritual things apart from God and His will. We Catholics have no desire for this and such things are forbidden by the Church anyway.

You see, we Catholics believe that death is truly conquered in the resurrection of Jesus Christ. We do not believe people in heaven are really dead. We believe they are living, and they are just as connected to the Holy Spirit as we are, if not more so. They are more finely attuned to what is happening in the Body of Christ than we are. Therefore, we can communicate with them. We can send messages to them, through the Holy Spirit in prayer, and we most certainly can ask them to pray for us, which is what we do. The real question is: why do some Christians **not** pray to Saints? Has not the power of death truly been conquered in the resurrection of Jesus Christ? Why do some Christians assert that the dead are truly dead and helpless when the Bible says they are not?[130] Perhaps the answer can be found in their refusal to pray to angels as well. They mistake prayer for worship.

[130] Hebrews 12:1; Revelation 5:8

Why do Catholics have statues of Mary and other Saints?

Statues, sculptures, carved reliefs and paintings of various figures from the Bible, and various holy persons throughout history, are called images, and they serve as visual reminders of these persons and the virtues they represent. They are used as visual aids in the same way a Bible serves as a written aid. When one enters a private home, it is common to see pictures of family members on the walls, both living and deceased. In the same way, when one enters a Catholic Church, the images of loved ones in the Church (heroes of the faith) are commonplace.[131]

Doesn't the Bible forbid the use of statues and "graven images?"

I certainly hope not, since a photograph of any kind would qualify as a "graven image" even if it is only graven with ink. You better toss those family photos if that's the case! The Biblical passage most commonly used to support the notion that graven images are forbidden by God is Exodus 20:4-5. However, just five chapters later, in Exodus 25:18-19, the very same God that supposedly forbade graven images, then commanded Moses to make graven images. So which is it? Are we to have graven images or not? Was God effectively saying; "*Make no graven images, except this one?*" Then in Numbers 21:8-9, God again commanded

[131] Catechism of the Catholic Church, paragraphs 1159 - 1162

Moses to make a graven image. Then in 1st Kings 6:23-29 and 1st Kings 7:25-45, we see that God actually blessed Solomon's Temple, made in God's honor, which was covered with graven images inside and out! Clearly, God does not have a problem with graven images; not statues, nor icons, nor paintings.

If we take a closer look at the context of the prohibition against graven images in Exodus 20, we can see that what God was really forbidding was the making of graven images *dedicated to false gods*. What God actually forbade was the worship of false gods, and any image that represented such false divinity. He was not prohibiting the creation and display of graven images in general. Nor did he forbid their use in places of worship dedicated to him. What God forbade was the creation of images that represent a deity (god or goddess) other than himself. For God is not only a jealous God, but he does not contradict himself either. It is illogical to say that God prohibits all graven images, but then commands and blesses the use of graven images. When reading the Bible, remember the Rule of Context, which is *context rules!* To say that God prohibits graven images because of one particular verse, and then just leave it at that, is a gross violation of the rule of context. God does not prohibit graven images! What he prohibits is graven images of false gods. There is a difference.

Why do Catholics believe in the ever virginity of Mary when the Bible talks about the "brothers" of Jesus Christ?

Jesus spoke Aramaic. The gospel was first proclaimed in Aramaic. In the ancient language of Aramaic, there is no word for cousin, aunt or uncle. These members of extended family are simply referred to as "brothers" and "sisters." The same is true of ancient Hebrew.[132]

The references in the New Testament that refer to the "brothers" and "sisters" of Jesus have no Biblical connection to actual blood siblings. In fact, the Scriptures refer to different mothers for some of those named as "brothers" of our Lord.[133] Of course many Evangelicals refer to a single word "*until*" in Matthew 1:25 to prove that Mary lost her virginity after the birth of Jesus Christ. They fail to recognize that the same word "*until*" is used multiple times in Scripture,[134] and in no way means something changed after a certain event.

Besides the unanimous Tradition of the early Church, what clearly tells us that Jesus had no male siblings, is the fact that when Jesus was dying on the cross, he gave care of his mother to his disciple John rather than to the next male sibling in line, as Jewish law would require, as well as the teaching of the Apostles, that widows (like Mary) are

[132] Genesis 14:12, 16

[133] Matthew 27:56; John 19:25

[134] Matthew 28:20; 1st Corinthians 15:25; 1st Timothy 4:13

to be cared for by their own family **first**.[135] Are we to believe that Jesus broke Jewish Law, and the Faith he taught his Apostles, immediately before he died? If he did, that would make him a sinner, and thus an imperfect sacrifice. No, Jesus did not (indeed he could not) break the Law of Moses, or his own teachings, because as a Jewish man he was under the Law of Moses, and as God he could not sin or contradict himself. So the fact that he gave the care of his mother to somebody who was clearly not his sibling brother indicates that he had no sibling brothers. To say that he did is to make Jesus Christ a self-contradicting sinner while he was on the cross dying for our sins.

Why do Catholics believe Mary was without sin?

Besides the unanimous consensus of the early Church, and plenty of early Christian writings to support that, dating back to the second century, the greeting of the Archangel Gabriel is the Biblical reference that clues us in. The angel Gabriel addressed Mary with the Greek word *kecharitomene* (κεχαριτωμένη), meaning "*full of grace*" – (Luke 1:28), not "*highly favored one*" as some modern English translations erroneously put it. The term "grace" does mean the favor of God, but to say that one is "full of grace" is to say that one has no room for sin. The implication of the Greek word *kecharitomene* is that Mary was gifted by God with the full measure of sanctifying grace. No more grace could be given because she was already "full."

[135] John 19:26-27; 1st Timothy 5:3-8; Deuteronomy 25:5; Deuteronomy 27:19

According to Scripture, Mary was already in the state of grace that Christians do not attain until after they receive justification in Christ. This has led the Catholic Church to understand that God created Mary in the same state of grace as he created Adam and Eve, and that by God's mercy, Mary was not stained with original sin like the rest of us.

Theologically, this is very important, because Jesus received all of his human flesh and blood from Mary. That flesh and blood ought to be unspoiled and unstained by sin. Furthermore, modern science tells us that cells from the mother and child do exchange between them during pregnancy. Jesus and Mary shared flesh and blood, as all mothers and their babies do during normal human pregnancy. That means for Jesus to inherit and maintain a perfect body from his mother, without sin, his physical mother should be without sin as well. While God can do anything he wants, it is only fitting and proper for things to be done this way, and the Scripture seems to support this with the angelic salutation "full of grace."

Some Christians believe that Mary "became without sin" when she accepted God's plan to deliver the Savior. However, the angelic greeting seems to indicate that her state of grace existed **<u>prior</u>** to her acceptance of God's messianic plan. So while some Christians believe Mary *became immaculate*[136] at the announcement by the archangel, Catholics believe she was *conceived immaculate* before she was born. This is what is meant by the *Immaculate Conception.*[137] All Christians become immaculate (without sin) upon their

[136] Immaculate: meaning "without sin"

[137] Catechism of the Catholic Church, paragraphs 490 - 493

baptism, which in many cases happens shortly after birth. Mary, however, seems to be the only Christian who was made immaculate (without sin) before her birth.

The debate about when Mary became immaculate (without sin), or "*full of grace*," has been long-standing in Christianity. What has not been debated, until recently, is the notion that she was not immaculate at all, indeed not "*full of grace*" but just "*highly favored*" instead, and remained with original sin during her pregnancy with Jesus and after. That is a recent Protestant phenomenon. Such a notion was foreign to the early Church and the first Christians.

The doctrine of the Immaculate Conception of Mary is rich in ancient Jewish symbolism. It's foreshadowed in the Old Testament with the Ark of the Covenant. Hebrews 9:4 tells us that the contents contained inside the Ark of the Covenant were; the stone tablets of the Law (the word of God), along with a jar of manna (bread from heaven) and Aaron's rod (a symbol of the holy priesthood). All of these are images foreshadowing Jesus Christ, who is the incarnate Word of God,[138] the Bread from Heaven[139] and our eternal High Priest.[140]

Now the Ark of the Covenant was consecrated to God and considered holy. It was not to be touched by a sinful man under penalty of death, and God himself had no problem exacting this penalty, even when a man touched it in an attempt to prevent it from falling.[141] This Old

[138] John 1:1-4,14
[139] John 6:31-65
[140] Hebrews 4:14
[141] 2nd Samuel 6:6-7; 1st Chronicles 13:9-10

Testament example is designed to illustrate that the ark, which carried the symbols of the Old Covenant, was just as holy as the Old Covenant itself.

Now as I said, the stone tablets, manna and rod were signs foreshadowing Jesus Christ. He is the New Covenant. Thus, the "ark" that carried him in her womb is holy too, just as the ark that carried the symbols that foreshadowed him was holy. Mary is the Ark of the New Covenant because she carried Jesus Christ in her womb. Jesus, who is the Word of God, the Bread of Life and our eternal High Priest, was carried for nine months inside the "ark" of Mary. She carried him in her arms and on her hip for another two years at least. If the ark of the Old Covenant was holy, then surely this "ark" of the New Covenant is even holier.

Do Catholics believe Mary ascended to Heaven like Jesus?

No. Jesus ascended to Heaven, not Mary. Mary was *assumed* into Heaven. There is a difference. The word *assumed* in this context means "taken" or "vanished," and the doctrine of the *Assumption* is deeply connected to the doctrine of the Immaculate Conception (see above). This comes directly from the Tradition of the early Church. (Remember, the "Bible Alone" doctrine is unbiblical – see Chapter 3.) Early Christians agreed universally that this happened at the end of Mary's life on earth, much in the same way Enoch[142] and Elijah[143] were assumed at the end of their lives.

Explaining that the Virgin Mary's death and entombment could not have happened without great pomp and circumstance, Epiphanius wrote in AD 377: "*If the Holy Virgin had died and was buried, her falling asleep would have been surrounded with honor, death would have found her pure, and her crown would have been a virginal one... Had she been martyred according to what is written: 'Thine own soul a sword shall pierce,' then she would shine gloriously among the martyrs, and her holy body would have been declared blessed; for by her, did light come to the world.*" – (Epiphanius, Panarion, 78:23) He was just pointing out the obvious. The early Church was obsessed with relics. The slightest thread from an apostle's coat was venerated as holy by the early Christians. Had Mary not been "taken" miraculously at the end of her life, the relics of her body, hair, bones and clothing would have been venerated in churches for centuries. This did not happen. It's as if, like Christ, nothing remained of her to venerate. Like Enoch and Elijah, she just vanished. Prior to the Protestant Reformation in the sixteenth century, no Christian debated that she vanished. What was debated was whether or not she died first.

In 1950, Pope Pius XII put the debate to rest in the Catholic Church by infallibly declaring that Mary was assumed into Heaven at the end of her life.[144]

---

[142] Genesis 5:24

[143] 2nd Kings 2:11

[144] Catechism of the Catholic Church, paragraphs 966 & 974

Why do Catholics give so much honor to Mary?

Throughout all of Christian history, Mary has been given the highest honor and respect. In the early Church she took on the role of Mother for all the faithful, and many writings from the earliest Christians give her great respect. The real question here is why do so many Evangelicals **not** give high honor to Mary? Mary prophesied about herself when she said: "*all generations shall call me blessed.*" – (Luke 1:48) Do you call her blessed? Do you do so regularly? If not, why not? Why are you directly contradicting what the Bible says you should do?

To understand Mary's blessedness, we need to understand where she stands in the Kingdom of God.

First and foremost, she is the "new Eve" in the sense that her "yes" to God[145] counters Eve's "no" to God.[146] Mary became the "new Eve" in the sense that she became mother of all those who trust in Jesus Christ, who is the "new Adam,"[147] and in doing so she effectively became the first Christian. Mary was the first human being to ever believe, trust and submit to the will of God through Jesus Christ. She was the first among all Christians. That alone is enough to give her more honor than any other Christian, but it doesn't stop there.

Second, Mary gave birth to our Savior Jesus Christ. She cared for him, fed him, nourished him, clothed him and cleaned him. She was our Savior's first teacher. Can you

[145] Luke 1:38

[146] Genesis 3:2-6

[147] 1st Corinthians 15:22, 45

imagine that? She was chosen to teach the Law of Moses to the one who gave us the Law of Moses. Thus, the young theologian who so impressed the scribes at the Temple[148] was originally instructed in theology by her!

As if that were not enough, it doesn't stop there. Third, before the start of Jesus' ministry, Mary told others to listen and obey him at the wedding feast at Cana.[149] Thus she became the first evangelist!

Wait, there's more. Fourth, when Jesus was dying on the cross, he gave the care of his mother to his Apostle St John. Now John was not his literal blood brother, and Jewish Law, as well as Christin teaching, would demand that the care of Jesus' mother go to the next male sibling in line. Jesus didn't do this because one didn't exist. Instead he gave the care of his mother to one of his Apostles, and in so doing he made her the mother of this Apostle.[150] If Mary was made the mother of the Apostle, she is by default the spiritual mother of all his disciples and of the whole Church.

Again, that should be enough, but there is more. Fifth and finally, Jesus was the King of the Jews, and because he is God incarnate, that makes him the King of kings as well. The Church is a Kingdom, in which Jesus is the King. There is, however, something about Jewish men that most people know. They love their mothers and they give their mothers high places of honor in their lives. Likewise, it is an ancient Jewish custom for good Jewish kings to place their mothers on the throne beside them. In other words, ever

[148] Luke 2:46-47
[149] John 2:5
[150] John 19:26-27

since the days of Solomon,[151] many Jewish kings have made their mothers (not their wives) their queens. Jesus is an unmarried Jew and he is a Jewish King. *So???* It's only natural to believe that Jesus made Mary his Queen in Heaven, as it suggests in Revelation 12:1. The Bible says we are all made royalty in Christ,[152] so it only stands to reason that Mary is all that much more so.

The honor and respect that we Catholic Christians give to Mary in no way diminishes the honor, respect and worship we give to Jesus Christ. If anything, it enhances it, because without Jesus Christ, Mary is nothing, and she would be the first one to tell us that.

[151] 1st Kings 2:29

[152] 1st Peter 2:9

CHAPTER 5: SALVATION

Are Catholics "saved" or "born again?"

Yes. However, we Catholic Christians don't look at this as a one-time event like many "born-again" Evangelicals do. While we believe we are "born again" through baptism (John 3:2-5),[153] which is the Biblical context of the saying "born again," we also believe in salvation as an ongoing process that is past, present and future. Yes, I ***was*** saved (Romans 8:24) at my baptism. Yes, I ***am being*** saved (Philippians 2:12) as I live my life in Christ. Yes, I believe I ***will be*** saved (Matthew 10:22) upon my death and when Christ returns.

We Catholics don't usually do one-time "altar calls" like Evangelicals, wherein the pastor asks people to come to the front of the chapel, say the "sinner's prayer" and publicly "give their hearts to Jesus Christ." Rather, we Catholics are asked to do the same thing every week by confessing the Creed[154] and receiving of the sacraments. When one receives the sacrament of the Holy *Eucharist* (Greek: "Thanksgiving") in Communion, one is asked to receive Jesus Christ. The same holds true in the sacrament of penance, wherein one says something similar to the sinner's prayer, as well as the other sacraments wherein Catholics rededicate their lives to Christ. For Catholics, "giving one's heart to Jesus Christ" is an ongoing process that never ends.

---

[153] Catechism of the Catholic Church, paragraphs 1212, 1215 - 1216

[154] Creed, usually the Nicene Creed or Apostles Creed, which is basically a statement of faith and confession of personal belief in the Trinity, Jesus Christ, redemption on the cross, his resurrection and second coming.

Do Catholics believe in salvation by faith alone?

No. We absolutely reject this concept because the Bible specifically contradicts it. The only place in the entire Bible where the phrase "faith alone" is found is in the Epistle of James which reads: *"You see that a man is justified by works and **not** by faith alone."* – (James 2:24)[155] There is no other passage in the Bible which suggests that "faith alone" is sufficient for salvation. There are plenty of verses that point out the superiority of faith over the old Mosaic Law,[156] but none of them say that salvation comes directly by "faith alone." These passages emphasise the fact that salvation is the work of God not man. It comes to us solely by God's grace (unmerited favor and mercy towards us), and we must receive that grace as a little baby receives the care of his mother.

St Paul pointed out that the Law of Moses was given as a tutor.[157] It was designed to teach us that we are sinners and we need God's grace. So that when we are old enough to have faith in God's grace we may do so, not trusting in our own righteousness. It was designed to teach us that our own righteousness is insufficient and that we can't be saved on our own – neither through our faith nor works. We need God to help us. That's what the Law of Moses was all about. Father Abraham understood this, and so God initiated in

[155] Revised Standard Version Catholic Edition (RSVCE)

[156] Romans 3:21-22; Romans 4:1-24; Galatians 3:16-18; Galatians 5:2-5; Ephesians 2:8-9

[157] Galatians 3:24-25

Abraham's offspring (the Hebrew nation) a tutoring process (Law of Moses) that would lead that nation, and all of humanity, to the same understanding. When we receive God's grace, it produces both faith and works in us.[158] Both faith and works are the byproduct of God's grace. They go hand-in-hand. As St James said: "*For even as the body without the spirit is dead; so also faith without works is dead.*" – (James 2:26)

This is why salvation is an ongoing thing. It is a process that is not complete until we die, and this is why St Paul told us: "*with fear and trembling* ***work out*** *your salvation.*" – (Philippians 2:12)[159] You see, we Catholics believe in salvation by grace alone[160] (not faith alone), yet grace must not be resisted, either before justification, by denying the gospel,[161] or after justification, by engaging in mortal sin.[162]

The notion of salvation by "faith alone" came to us from the German reformer Martin Luther, as one of his "five solas" of German Protestant religion. It became extremely popular in the Protestant world. Luther himself could find no direct Biblical validation of this teaching, so he created one. In AD 1522, he artificially inserted the word "alone" after the word "faith" into Romans 3:23 of his German translation of the New Testament, thus changing the entire meaning of the text. Luther not only attempted to

[158] Catechism of the Catholic Church, paragraphs 2001 - 2005

[159] Emphasis mine

[160] Catechism of the Catholic Church, paragraphs 1996 - 2000

[161] Luke 12:10

[162] 1st John 5:16

remove some books from both the Old and New Testaments (see Chapter 3), but he also had no problem changing the text of Scripture itself to suit his theological presumptions. The Catholic Church does not permit the changing of Scripture to suit theological presumptions.

As Catholics we do not believe we "earn" our way to heaven as if we did not need the merits of Christ.[163] Far from it! We believe that everything we have comes directly from the grace of God, and this includes our salvation, our faith ***and*** our works.

Do Catholics believe in "once saved, always saved?"

No. The Scriptures are clear that one can lose his salvation if one rejects the forgiveness of God, either by persisting in unbelief or else persisting in mortal sin without repentance.[164]

Why do Catholics baptize babies when they can't even understand what is going on?

We Catholics baptize our infant children because Jesus said: "*Suffer the little children, and forbid them not to come to*

[163] "If any one saith, that man may be justified before God by his own works, whether done through the teaching of human nature, or that of the law, without the grace of God through Jesus Christ; let him be anathema." – (Council of Trent, Sixth Session, Canon I, AD 1547)
[164] Matthew 7:21; Matthew 24:13; Romans 11:22; 1st Corinthians 9:27; 1st Corinthians 10:11-12; 2nd Corinthians 11:15; Galatians 5:4; 2nd Timothy 2:11-13; Hebrews 6:4-6; Hebrews 10:26-27; Philemon 2:12; 1st Peter 1:9; Revelation 20:12-13

me: for the kingdom of heaven is for such." – (Matthew 19:14) St Peter told us that salvation comes through baptism.[165] We also baptize them because Saint Paul has specifically told us that baptism replaces circumcision as our initiation into covenant with God.[166] Jews circumcise their boys at eight days of age, to initiate them into the covenant God made with Moses. God didn't have a problem bringing babies into his covenant of the Law? Why would he have a problem bringing babies into his covenant of Grace?

As pointed out above, we Catholics do not believe in salvation by "faith alone," so faith is not necessary to receive God's grace when one is too young to understand or believe. An infant child just receives, and this is the example God wants all of his followers to understand about how salvation works. It's totally God's doing, not ours! We are expected to participate (cooperate) in our salvation (by faith and works) when we are old enough to do so, but it is neither our "faith alone," nor our "works alone," that saves us. Nor is it our "faith plus works" that saves us. It is God's grace and God's grace alone – period. There is no better example than that of an infant child receiving the sacrament of baptism to illustrate this. The child can do nothing, neither believe nor work. All the child can do is receive God's grace, and so that is what the child does.[167] That is what we must understand. God is our salvation – not us.

The early Christians baptized their infants and children and we have records of this going back as far as the

[165] 1st Peter 3:21

[166] Colossians 2:11-12

[167] Catechism of the Catholic Church, paragraphs 1216, 1250 - 1252

second century. The notion that children should not be baptized, because they are not old enough to express faith, did not come about until after the Protestant Reformation in the sixteenth century, and probably derives from the false notion that salvation comes through "faith alone." Indeed, if salvation came through "faith alone" then there would be no way anyone, too young to express faith, could be saved, or initiated into God's covenant made through Jesus Christ. So it would be wrong to baptize them. Thus, according to some Protestant rationale, babies who die in infancy would have no assurance of salvation whatsoever, since they would not have ever attained an age in which they can express faith. Again, this is probably the result of the "faith alone" misunderstanding. Because of this, many Protestants have come up with the "age of reason" idea to answer the unsettling thought that God would send unbaptized and unbelieving children to hell. For this reason, a few Protestants have even rejected the idea of original sin altogether.

These notions however, have no basis in Scripture. Since we know that salvation does not come by "faith alone" (see above), then we know that the covenant of salvation in Christ can certainly be presented to an infant through baptism, or a child of any age, just as the covenant of the Law in Moses was presented to infant males through circumcision on their eighth day. The Catholic message on baptism is the same as the Jewish message on circumcision. Don't wait! Initiate your children into God's covenant as quickly as possible, both for their benefit and yours.[168]

[168] Catechism of the Catholic Church, paragraph 1250

Do Catholics believe purgatory is a place between heaven and hell?

Actually, we Catholics don't believe that, and the Church doesn't teach that. In spite of all the myth and speculation that swirls around the topic of purgatory, the Church only officially teaches two things about it.[169]

One, it exists.[170] Two, our prayers and sacrifices help those who go there.[171] Now beyond that, it's just a matter of explaining what it is.

Explanations have changed a bit over the centuries as societies understand things in different ways, just as explanations of heaven and hell have changed over the centuries too. The first thing we need to understand about purgatory is that it's not an "in between" state of heaven and hell. Quite the opposite is true actually. Purgatory is connected to heaven in some sense. Some might even call it "*heaven's front door*." The only people who go to purgatory are people who are already saved, and the reason why they go to purgatory (or more accurately "through" purgatory), on their way to heaven, is to let the merits of Christ's atoning sacrifice burn away all of their sinful attachments to this present world.[172] This is so all that which is pure and holy in their lives may shine more brightly in the glory of heaven. That's basically it. It's the final method through which God

[169] Catechism of the Catholic Church, paragraphs 1030 - 1032

[170] Matthew 5:26; Matthew 12:32; 1st Peter 3:18-20 & 4:6

[171] 2nd Maccabees 12:44-46; 1st Corinthians 15:29-30; 2nd Timothy 1:16-18

[172] 1st Corinthians 3:11-15

takes imperfect people at the end of their lives, and through the merits of Christ, transforms them into perfect and glorified Saints in Heaven.

Do Catholics believe Evangelicals can be saved?

The answer is essentially yes. You see, Catholics and Evangelicals are united together by virtue of their common baptism in the name of the Holy Trinity.[173] Every baptism performed in the name of the Holy Trinity – Father, Son and Holy Spirit – is essentially a Catholic baptism, and every Evangelical church performs baptism this way. So that means that every baptized Evangelical has essentially received a Catholic baptism, regardless of who performed it, or where it was performed, and the Catholic Church fully recognizes this. This is why the Catholic Church does not attempt to "re-baptize" Evangelical converts, mainstream Protesant converts, or any Christian converts to the Catholic Church. So long as the original baptism was in the Name of the Trinity, it's considered legitimate and Catholic.

So right from the start, Evangelicals are initiated into the New Covenant of salvation in Jesus Christ in a fully Catholic way. After that, things start to change. Evangelicals have their own beliefs and practices which range far and wide, depending on which denomination or affiliation we're talking about.

[173] Catechism of the Catholic Church, paragraphs 818 - 819

The Catholic Church teaches that "*there is no salvation outside of the Church*"[174] and by this it means sacramental membership through baptism, not necessarily official membership on paper. The Catholic Church also recognizes the gifts of the Holy Spirit operating within non-Catholic churches, and officially considers Evangelicals (and all Protestants) to be "fellow Christians" by virtue of their Trinitarian baptism.[175]

Where Evangelicals enter a precarious position is when it comes to their knowledge of the Catholic Church. Those who are ignorant of the Catholic Church's essential role in salvation history cannot be held accountable for what they don't know. However, those who have studied history, and the teachings of the Catholic Church (as highlighted in this book), knowing the essential role the Catholic Church plays in salvation history, will be held accountable to God for what they know at their judgement.[176] It is a cause for fear and trembling before God Almighty. With knowledge comes responsibility. Evangelicals who have studied, and know the truth about the Catholic Church, must seek reconciliation with the Catholic Church. We all must follow the convictions of a well-informed conscience.

Do Catholics believe in the Rapture?

Understanding that this is an important issue for many Evangelicals, equating to salvation for some, the short

[174] Catechism of the Catholic Church, paragraph 846

[175] Catechism of the Catholic Church, paragraph 1271

[176] Catechism of the Catholic Church, paragraph 846

answer is "no," Catholics do not believe in the Rapture the same way most Evangelicals do. Of course, Catholics do believe in the Second Coming of Jesus Christ,[177] and Catholics do believe the Scriptures that say all his followers (both living and dead) will rise up in the air to meet him on that Last Day.[178] However, there is nothing in Scripture that says believers will be spared the Tribulation of the Last Days and be "raptured" (taken up into heaven) prior to it. This is a novel interpretation invented in the 1800s by John Nelson Darby, former Anglican priest and co-founder of the Plymouth Brethren. No Christian held to this view prior to him.

In the early twentieth century, Darby's novel ideas were placed into the margins of the Scofield Reference Bible by one of Darby's disciples, Cyrus I Scofield. This Bible became very popular in Evangelicals seminaries due to its many cross-references and footnotes. Basically, it was put together very well and highly useful. However, it contained Darby's Rapture theory peppered throughout. This is how an obscure and novel interpretation, of the Second Coming of Christ, became a mainstream Evangelical doctrine.

The Catholic understanding of the Last Days is very simple, following the teachings of the Early Church and most of the Early Church Fathers. When the Last Days come, the world will come under the influence of the Antichrist, leading people into a great apostasy against Jesus

---

177 Apostles Creed; Nicene Creed; Catechism of the Catholic Church, paragraphs 673-679, 997-1004

178 1st Thessalonians 4:13-18; 1st Thessalonians 5:1-8; 1st Corinthians 15:50-58

Christ and his Catholic Church. This Antichrist will persecute true Christians and set up a false religion, naming himself as Christ and God. When it appears that all is lost, Jesus Christ will return in the clouds and the heavens will be split open. The dead will rise, and those Christians who remain alive will be transformed. Both the resurrected dead in Christ, and the transformed living in Christ, will rise together to meet Christ in the air as he returns to earth for the final judgement, and the restoration of all things for eternity. Some Evangelical scholars might classify the Catholic understanding of Last Days eschatology as "amillennial, post-tribulation rapture."[179]

[179] "Amillennial" refers to a non-literal interpretation of the one-thousand-year period described in Revelation 20:1-7, which is often understood as a symbolic representation of the Church Age, from the time of the Early Church to the time of the Antichrist. "Post-tribulation rapture" means the resurrection of the dead, and the transformation of the living in Christ, does not happen until after the tribulation of Antichrist.

CHAPTER 6: THE SACRAMENT

Do Catholics really believe that communion bread and wine become the literal flesh and blood of Jesus Christ?

Yes, because Jesus said so. Have you ever read John 6:66? In addition to the apocalyptic connection to this number, it's the most frightening verse in the whole Bible. It reads: "*Because of this many of his disciples turned back and no longer went about with him.*" – (John 6:66)[180] What was the context of this passage? Jesus just finished explaining to his disciples the mystery of Holy Communion.[181] He described himself as the "*bread of life,*" and just when you think Jesus was pulling one of those non-literal parables again, he kicks it up a notch, and goes straight into literal speech. He told his disciples that they must literally *"eat"* his flesh and "*drink*" his blood to have eternal life. Jesus told his disciples that this is spiritual[182] (as in not carnal) but that it is literal too. Read these passages over and over again to see for yourself. Many of his disciples left him after this. He didn't go after them and say: "*Wait! I wasn't speaking literally. You misunderstood.*" It would be cruel to suggest that Jesus deliberately mislead his disciples to drive them away with a

---

[180] Revised Standard Version Catholic Edition (RSVCE)

[181] John 6:51-65

[182] Spiritual doesn't mean "metaphorical" as some mistakenly think. It means "other worldly" and "supernatural" (above nature). Angels are spiritual beings. They are other worldly, but they are real. They are not metaphors.

symbolic parable that he allowed them to misunderstand as literal. No. Jesus Christ was speaking literally here, and he was allowing his own disciples to leave him because of it.

Now since the earliest days of Christianity, well documented all the way back to the early second century,[183] the Church has always taught that when the priest consecrates the communion bread and wine, these elements literally become the body and blood of Jesus Christ, hidden supernaturally under the mere *physical appearance* of bread and wine.[184] Saint Ignatius of Antioch, writing in about AD 105, said the following about those who did not believe this to be literal: *"Heretics abstain from the Eucharist and from prayer, because they do not confess that the Eucharist is the flesh of our Savior Jesus Christ."* – (Ignatius, Letter to the Smyrnaeans 6) This same Ignatius, who was the Bishop of Antioch and ordained by the Apostle John, was shortly thereafter martyred in the Colosseum at Rome, where he was fed to lions before a cheering crowd. He died for his faith in Christ, the whole faith, even the part about eating the literal flesh, and drinking the literal blood, of Jesus Christ.

When we say the bread and wine literally become the body and blood of Jesus Christ, what we mean to say is that both species contain all of the properties of Jesus Christ. The bread literally becomes the body of Jesus Christ. The wine literally becomes the blood. Now, Jesus Christ is living, and therefore his body and blood cannot be separated. So to

---

[183] Ignatius of Antioch, Epistle to Smyrnaeans, 7:1 (AD 105); Justin Martyr, First Apology, 66 (AD 110-165); Irenaeus, Against Heresies, IV:18,4 (AD 200)

[184] Catechism of the Catholic Church, paragraphs 1375 - 1376

partake of just one species is to partake of the whole and complete Christ[185] – body and blood, humanity, together with his soul and divinity.[186] When we look at all the Biblical passages dealing with communion,[187] not a single one suggests a non-literal interpretation is in order. Not a single one gives us a "symbolic" or "metaphorical" context. It's all very literal and straightforward. Remember, the first rule of Biblical interpretation is the Rule of Context, which states that *context rules!* The context in John 6 is literal. Don't take my word for it. Read it, and see for yourself.

So does this mean that Catholics believe Jesus is re-crucified every time a priest says the Mass?

No. We believe the Eucharist is the living and resurrected Christ that is made present to us,[188] who was once crucified, once and for all time,[189] not to be misunderstood as to say that Christ is somehow re-sacrificed, re-crucified, re-killed or re-murdered every time we celebrate the Holy Mass.[190] That would be both blasphemy and nonsense. No, the communion we receive is the living and resurrected Jesus Christ who was slain once,

[185] Catechism of the Catholic Church, paragraph 1390

[186] Catechism of the Catholic Church, paragraph 1374

[187] Matthew 26:26-28; Mark 14:22-24; Luke 22:19-20; 1st Corinthians 10:16; 1st Corinthians 11:23-29

[188] Catechism of the Catholic Church, paragraph 1373

[189] Catechism of the Catholic Church, paragraph 1366

[190] Catechism of the Catholic Church, paragraph 1545

resurrected and now shares himself supernaturally with us. The sacrifice was offered (slain) 2,000 years ago, but has been re-presented and consumed ever since.

Do Catholics believe Protestant communion is the same as Catholic communion?

No. This is because we believe the authority to ask God to bring about the transubstantiation of the communion elements was given by Jesus Christ to his Apostles, who in turn gave it to the bishops and priests they chose. This authority is passed down through generations in a specific and defined line of succession which can be easily traced through history back to the Apostles. In order for a transubstantiation of the communion elements to occur, a minister must be properly ordained by a bishop who has this authentic Apostolic succession back to the Apostles. Protestant ministers (most especially Evangelical pastors) do not have this, and most would not dare to claim it. So they cannot call on God for transubstantiation of the communion elements. For most Protestants, communion means something altogether different than it does for Catholics.

So then is Protestant communion just symbolic?

For most Protestants (especially Evangelicals), when they celebrate communion, it really is just a symbolic meal of remembrance, similar to the Jewish Passover Seder. While there are a few Mainline Protestant ministers here and there (perhaps some Anglicans and Scandinavian Lutherans) who may actually have legitimate Apostolic succession, the overwhelming vast majority of Protestant ministers do not, nor do they claim to have it. This is especially true for Evangelical pastors. So for them, nothing really happens at the consecration portion of the service, assuming the communion elements are consecrated at all. In some Evangelical churches they are not.

Because of this, some Evangelical churches put the emphasis on everyone in the congregation receiving the communion elements at the exact same time. This is their understanding of "communion." It's more of a communion with each other, in their spiritual and baptismal union in Christ. Thus, the bread and wine (often grape juice) are distributed in small plastic cups in advance, while everyone waits for the pastor to give the cue. At that moment, all receive the elements together simultaneously, in symbolic unison, as they communally remember the last supper of Jesus Christ.

This is considerably different from the Catholic practice of Holy Communion which is understood to be literal. In Catholic churches, the emphasis is on the individual reception of the real presence of God in the communion elements. The word "communion" then takes on a much deeper meaning, in that the communicant is literally having physical contact with God the Son – Jesus Christ – under the accidental appearance of bread and wine.

So if Catholics believe the communion elements are literally the manifestation of Jesus Christ, who is God, does that mean that

Catholics worship these communion elements as God?

Yes. The communion elements, called the Holy Eucharist, once consecrated, have become the literal body, blood, soul and divinity of Jesus Christ, hidden under the mere physical appearance (accidents) of bread and wine. We Catholics worship this real physical presence of Jesus Christ in the Holy Eucharist.[191]

How is the Catholic worship of bread and wine not idolatry?

Well, if it were only "bread and wine," then it really would be idolatry, but it's not merely "bread and wine." It's the real and literal presence of Jesus Christ (God the Son) made manifest under the accidental appearance of bread and wine. So when Catholics worship this Holy Eucharist, we are worshipping the literal and physical presence of Jesus Christ. Many Catholics, myself included, whisper the words of St Thomas the Apostle at the consecration and elevation of the communion elements: "*My Lord, and my God.*" – (John 20:28) It is fitting that these words came from "doubting Thomas" when he finally realized the truth and believed. Every Catholic, especially an Evangelical convert like myself, has this Thomistic epiphany when he finally realizes what Jesus was talking about in John 6:51-65. This communion Eucharist, which just looks like ordinary bread and wine, really and truly is the risen Lord Jesus Christ! You see, it's just a matter of taking Jesus at his word. He said it, I believe

[191] Catechism of the Catholic Church, paragraphs 1378 & 1418

it, and that settles it. The real question here is this; if he said it, and you don't believe it, why not?

How can this Catholic worship of communion elements be Biblical?

Worship usually involves sacrifice. It has always involved sacrifice since the first recorded act of worship in the Bible (Genesis 4:4). Under the Old Covenant, unblemished animals were brought to the Temple for sacrifice,[192] and ancient Jews would worship God as these animals were being sacrificed to him. Then, especially during the Passover sacrifice, the meat from this animal holocaust was given back to the Jewish worshipper, and roasted in fire for consumption in the Passover Seder meal. Thus, every Jewish sacrifice had two parts, the offering and the consumption. The offering happened only once, when the animal was killed. The consumption happened multiple times, as the worshipper ate the Passover lamb, one bite after another, sharing it with others in his family, and then going back for seconds and thirds, until all of the meat was gone.[193]

This illustrates communion in the Catholic understanding of Jesus Christ as God's Passover Lamb. The offering of this sacrifice of Christ happened only once, on the cross at Calvary. The consumption happens many times, millions of times actually, in Eucharistic liturgies all over the globe, century after century, until this present day. However, like the loaves of bread and fish that were multiplied in the

[192] Leviticus 1:1 through Leviticus 9:24
[193] Exodus 12:1-11; Numbers 9:9-13

gospels,[194] this sacrificial consumption never runs out. Miraculously, it continues indefinitely until the end of time, when all who participate have been filled with the physical presence of Jesus Christ.

As stated above, true worship usually involves a sacrifice combined with adoration – the complete submission of the body, mind, soul and will. This is what Catholics are doing in the holy liturgy of the Mass. This is worship in a Biblical sense. Prayer by itself is not worship. Praise and song by themselves are not worship. However, when these things are combined with a real "flesh and blood" sacrifice, and the full submission of our bodies, minds, souls and will, we have authentic Biblical worship, which is identical to that of the Hebrew patriarchs, ancient Israel and the early Church.

How can any reasonable and sane person be expected to believe such absurdity as the transubstantiation of bread and wine into the literal flesh and blood of Jesus Christ?

Remember John 6:66? From the very beginning, many have left the company of Jesus and his Apostles (the true and authentic Church) over this teaching. When you really stop and think about it, taking Jesus' words at face value, over the transubstantiation, is no more absurd than many of the other miracles the Bible records. Do you believe Moses parted the Red Sea? Do you believe God stopped the sun for Joshua? Do you believe Jonah was swallowed and

[194] Matthew 14:13-21

vomited by a giant fish? Do you believe Jesus walked on water? Do you believe Jesus healed the sick and raised the dead? Do you believe that he himself rose from the dead and ascended into heaven? If you can believe such "absurd" things as these, how hard can it be to believe a properly consecrated Eucharist (communion bread and wine) is the literal flesh and blood of Jesus Christ? Especially since he said it is.

CHAPTER 7: THE CHURCH

Do Catholics really believe the Catholic Church is the one and only Church ever established by Jesus Christ?

Yes, we most certainly do. This is based both on the Biblical record and historical evidence. The term "Catholic" is Greek – *katholikos* (καθολικός) – and means "whole, universal and complete." The term "Catholic Church" has been used since the late first-century to contrast the Church of the Apostles with false heretical sects that were springing up among the Judaizers and Greek Gnostics.

In AD 105, Saint Ignatius of Antioch wrote the following to the Christians in Smyrna: "*See that you all follow the bishop, even as Jesus Christ does the Father, and the presbytery* [priests] *as you would the Apostles; and reverence the deacons, as being the institution of God. Let no man do anything connected with the Church without the bishop. Let that be deemed a proper Eucharist, which is* [administered] *either by the bishop, or by one* [priest] *to whom he has entrusted it. Wherever the bishop shall appear, there let the multitude also be;* ***even as, wherever Jesus Christ is, there is the Catholic Church***." – (Ignatius, Letter to the Smyrnaeans 8) Now this Ignatius of Antioch was a bishop in the early Church who was ordained by the Apostle John himself, and was martyred at the Colosseum in Rome. Ignatius, disciple of the Apostle John, died for Jesus Christ and the Church he called "Catholic." Let that sink in.

We believe the Catholic Church is the messianic Kingdom of God, promised to ancient Israel, and is indeed the heir of ancient Israel.[195] In fact, in the Greek version of the Old Testament (*Septuagint*), ancient Israel is referred to many times as *ecclesia* (ἐκκλησία) or "the Church." The New Testament Church (*ecclesia*) is just a continuation of that. Jesus Christ is the King of Israel, and therefore the King of the Catholic Church. This Kingdom/Church was established between AD 30-33, when King Jesus made Peter his prime minister: "*Simon Peter answered and said: Thou art Christ, the Son of the living God. And Jesus answering, said to him: Blessed art thou, Simon Bar-Jona: because flesh and blood hath not revealed it to thee, but my Father who is in heaven. And I say to thee: That thou art Peter; and upon this rock I will build my church, and the gates of hell shall not prevail against it. And I will give to thee the keys of the kingdom of heaven. And whatsoever thou shalt bind upon earth, it shall be bound also in heaven: and whatsoever thou shalt loose upon earth, it shall be loosed also in heaven.*" – (Matthew 16:16-19) [196] Ever since then, this Catholic Church has been established, and it was inaugurated at the Feast of Pentecost following the death and resurrection of Jesus Christ.

At this point the leadership of ancient Israel ceased to be the scribes, priests and pharisees. From that time forward, the true and authentic leadership of Israel was found in the Apostles appointed by King Jesus. Historical records tell us that in about AD 42,[197] the King's prime minister (St Peter) travelled from Antioch to Rome, and there he established his permanent *Apostolic See* (meaning a

[195] Catechism of the Catholic Church, paragraphs 751, 761-766 & 877

[196] Emphasis mine

[197] Irenaeus, Against Heresies, 3:1:1 (AD 180); Eusebius of Caesarea, The Chronicle (AD 303)

seat of authority). It was at this time, the Catholic Church became the "Roman Catholic Church" because Peter was now in Rome. Later, St Paul arrived in Rome, and together the two built the Church of Rome into the headquarters of ancient Christianity. Saints Peter and Paul were martyred in Rome in AD 67. St Paul was beheaded and St Peter was crucified upside-down. His body was placed in the catacombs beneath *Mons Vaticanus*, just outside the old city and across the Tiber, where the Vatican is today. Since then, Peter's direct successors (the popes) have carried on the ministry of St Peter, having inherited through ordination and consecration the same Apostolic authority once held by St Peter.

So do Catholics believe Evangelical churches are illegitimate?

That depends on what you mean by the word "churches." Catholics believe that Jesus Christ established only one Church – the Catholic Church – but the word "church" is used many ways in the English language. It could refer to the whole company of Christian believers around the world. It could refer to a small group of Christian believers in a local area. Or it could refer to an actual chapel structure in which Christian worship is celebrated. All of these are legitimate uses of the word "church" in the English language.

Now, when it comes to how these churches were established, that's a totally different matter. Catholics understand Jesus as having established one institutional Church upon Peter (the "rock") and that this institutional

Church subsists entirely in those local churches, around the world, in full-communion with the successor of St Peter (the "patriarch of Rome" who is also called "the pope"). This One, Holy, Catholic and Apostolic Church is considered whole and complete in and of itself.[198]

Now, that being said, the Catholic Church does fully acknowledge the presence of Christians outside of this institutional structure, who may be united to it through the sacrament of Trinitarian baptism,[199] but for whatever reasons have been separated (in diaspora) from visible union with the pope. Likewise, these Christians have, in many cases, organized themselves into their own visible communities wherein the gifts of the Holy Spirit are clearly in operation in some limited capacity. The Holy Spirit uses these communities as a means of salvation, but they derive their power from the fullness of grace that Jesus Christ gave to the Catholic Church.[200] It's their connection to Catholic truth that makes them a means of grace for the salvation of souls. In other words, the likelihood these non-Catholic communities will be used by God, is entirely dependent on how closely they follow the core of Catholic teaching and practice.

From the very beginning, men have taken it upon themselves to call upon the name of Jesus outside of the institutional Church Jesus established. While this has never been Christ's will, Jesus likewise did not condemn them for

[198] Catechism of the Catholic Church, paragraph 820

[199] Catechism of the Catholic Church, paragraph 818

[200] Catechism of the Catholic Church, paragraph 819

it,[201] especially if they didn't know any better. If anything, the operation of the Holy Spirit in these other communities is a call for Catholic unity among Christians, and indeed that was the desire of Christ all along. For he plainly told his Apostles, on the night before he died, that any lack of Catholic unity among Christians would be a scandal and a hindrance to effective evangelism of the unsaved.[202]

These non-Catholic, but Christian, communities may not have been established by Jesus Christ, therefore they are not "The Church" in the proper understanding of the word, but they can nevertheless be "a church" or "churches" in another linguistic sense, so as to say real Christian "communities." While it would be improper to call these churches "illegitimate," because they are clearly legitimate gatherings of Christians, it is only fair and honest to understand that they are not the institutional "Church" established by Jesus Christ in AD 33.

How can Catholics say that Peter is the "rock" upon which Jesus built the Church, when clearly the passage used to support this uses two completely different words for "rock?"

In Matthew 16, the Greek word used for Peter is *petros* (πέτρος) while the Greek word used for the rock Jesus said he would build his Church on is *petra* (πέτρα). These are two completely different words. "Petros" means little stone, while "petra" means huge boulder. "*And I say to thee: That*

[201] Mark 9:38-41
[202] John 17:20-21

thou art [Petros]*; and upon this* [petra] *I will build my church.*" – (Matthew 16:18)[203]

The problem here is the Greek language. You see, in Greek, words are inflected with gender. So *petros* is inflected with a male gender, while *petra* is inflected with a female gender. We see similar gender inflection in many other languages too. Now because these two Greek words have a different gender, and because they mean two different things, it has led some Protestant theologians to teach that while Jesus gave the name "rock" *petros* (πέτρος) to Simon Bar-Jona, he did so symbolically, because he was **really** talking about a completely different symbolic "rock" *petra* (πέτρα) which they say was the revelation that Simon gave – that Jesus is the messianic Son of God. The problem with this interpretation is that it's linguistically impossible and out of context. These Protestant theologians have fallen victim to the old language trap.

The Greek version of the Gospel of Matthew is a translation from an original Aramaic text. One of the early Church Fathers, Irenaeus, wrote the following in about AD 180: "*Matthew also issued a written Gospel among the Hebrews in their own dialect, while Peter and Paul were preaching at Rome, and laying the foundations of the Church.*" – (Irenaeus, Against Heresies 3:1) What was the dialect of the Hebrews during that time? It was Aramaic. So based on Irenaeus' testimony, we know the first (and original) version of Matthew's gospel was written in Aramaic not Greek. So what many Protestants are relying upon, to make their argument that

[203] Greek clarification mine

Peter is not the rock, is actually a translation of Matthew's text, not the original text itself.

Here's what logically happened. The Greek translator of this Aramaic text ran into a problem with the Aramaic word for "rock" in reference to the name Jesus gave to Simon. The obvious Greek translation for the "rock," upon which Jesus would build his Church, is *petra*, meaning a large boulder, but the problem is that in Greek, *petra* is a girl's name! You can't give Peter a girl's name!!! The masculine form, *petros*, works as a proper boy's name, but means "little stone," and doesn't convey the massive character of the "rock" that Jesus built his Church upon. The Greek translator of Matthew's gospel was simply trying to make Matthew's plain Aramaic statement, about Peter being the "rock," work in the Greek language.

The truth is, Jesus didn't name Simon "*Petros*" at all! In fact, there is no evidence that Jesus ever spoke Greek on a regular basis. Jesus was a Jew who lived in the Galilee region of Palestine. He spoke Aramaic, as all Jews in that area did at that time, with perhaps a smattering of Hebrew, which was at that time nearly an extinct language, spoken exclusively in the Temple in Jerusalem. However, Hebrew was not the language Jesus spoke in public settings. Instead, he used Aramaic, because that's what everyone else understood, and if St Matthew's intended audience was the Jews (as every Biblical scholar affirms) then of course he would write it in Aramaic. The majority of the world's Jewish population was living in Palestine at that time, and they spoke Aramaic not Greek. It's very clear, based on both tradition and history, that the name Jesus gave to Simon Bar-Jonah was not the Greek word for "rock" (*petros*) but rather the Aramaic word for rock *cephas* (Aramaic: כיפא, or Greek spelling: Κηφας), and this is backed with Scripture.[204] Now the Aramaic word *cephas* means "rock." It neither means big rock nor little rock, and it's neither male nor female. It just means "rock." In Aramaic, Jesus would have said: "*And I say to thee: That thou art* [Cephas]*; and upon this* [cephas] *I will build my church.*" – (Matthew 16:18)[205] It's really very simple you see, and it's contextual, because of what Jesus said in his next breath: "*And I will give to thee the keys of the kingdom of heaven. And whatsoever thou shalt bind upon earth, it shall be bound also in heaven: and whatsoever thou shalt loose upon earth, it shall be loosed also in heaven.*" – (Matthew 16:19)

What did Jesus do here? Simple. He gave Peter (Cephas) the promise of authority, real spiritual authority, the authority to "bind and loose," meaning the authority to define doctrine and law within the Church, which will be backed by the force of Heaven itself! Jesus was doing what every king always does. He was investing authority into his prime minister. In the Old Testament, we see a similar pattern, with similar terminology, wherein King Hezekiah appointed Eliakim as his prime minister using a "key" as a symbol of his authority.[206] Here, in Matthew's gospel, King Jesus is doing the same, following the same Biblical pattern. A Jewish audience, in first century Palestine, would have immediately picked up on this.

[204] John 1:42; 1st Corinthians 1:12; 1st Corinthians 15:5; Galatians 2:9; etc.

[205] Aramaic clarification mine

[206] Isaiah 22:20-22

How can Peter (Cephas) be the "rock" when the Apostle Paul calls Jesus Christ the "rock?"

St Paul, the Apostle, refers to Jesus Christ as the "rock" in his first epistle to the Corinthians, which says: "*And all drank the same spiritual drink; (and they drank of the spiritual rock that followed them, and the rock was Christ).*" – (1st Corinthians 10:4) He even uses the feminine Greek word *petra* (πέτρα) to do this. However, this is easily answered in the historical fact that Paul wrote his epistles in Greek. Unlike Matthew's gospel, he did not originally write in Aramaic. The most commonly used words for "rock" available in Greek were *petra* (πέτρα) and *petros* (πέτρος). So Paul used the feminine word *petra* (πέτρα), meaning "large boulder," to describe Jesus Christ in a spiritual sense. Notice he did not name Jesus *petra*. That would be disrespectful and blasphemous to give the Son of God a girl's name. He just used the word to describe him metaphorically. There are other similar references to God in both the Old and New Testaments. They are completely unrelated to Matthew 16:18, which was originally written in Aramaic, wherein Jesus actually renamed Simon to *Cephas* (Aramaic: כיפא), meaning "rock," and said he would build his Church upon this *Cephas*.

How can Catholics say Peter died in Rome, when there is no Biblical record of Peter ever being in Rome?

Just because something is not written plainly in the Book of Acts doesn't mean it didn't happen. It's astonishing that so many modern Evangelicals assert this when the historical records are indisputable, and no early Christian writer even questioned that both Peter and Paul died in Rome.

For example, St Ignatius of Antioch, on his journey to himself be martyred in Rome, in AD 105, wrote to the Roman Christians, urging them not to lobby for his release, saying: "*I issue you no commands, like Peter and Paul: they were Apostles, while I am but a captive.*" – (Ignatius of Antioch, Epistle to the Romans, 4) Thus, he indicated the position of authority Peter and Paul held in Rome during their residence there. Irenaeus, in about AD 180, summarised the position of the early Roman Church in ancient Christianity as follows: "*the very great, the very ancient, and universally known Church founded and organized at Rome by the two most glorious Apostles, Peter and Paul; as also the faith preached to men, which comes down to our time by means of the successions of the bishops. For it is a matter of necessity that every Church should agree with this Church, on account of its preeminent authority, that is, the faithful everywhere, inasmuch as the tradition has been preserved continuously by those who exist everywhere.*" – (Irenaeus, Against Heresies 3:2) This is just but a small example of the writings of the ancients who universally asserted, and never denied, the presence of Peter and Paul in Rome, and even more so, asserted that because of their presence in Rome, the Roman Church had a position of preeminence in the ancient world.

In addition to that, it's a mistake to say that there is no Biblical record of Peter ever living in Rome. Indeed there is. The Bible contains one of the letters written by St Peter to the Christians in Asia Minor. Here, it would appear that Peter was writing to some of the Christians he once shepherded in that area around Antioch. At the end of this short epistle he sends his farewell: "*The church that is in Babylon, elected together with you, saluteth you: and so doth my son Mark.*" – (1st Peter 5:13)

The reference to Mark as a "son" again demonstrates the paternal nature of Christian leaders as "fathers" in the early Church (see Chapter 2). Indeed, what else could Mark call Peter but "Father?"

The only question that remains is: where is this "Babylon" Peter speaks of? It's certainly not the literal Babylon in present day Iraq. During St Peter's time, that city was a ghost town and was only very sparsely populated. There is no record of St Peter ever going there, and indeed, there would be no reason for him to go there.

Peter's Apostolic journey led him out of Jerusalem up north to Galilee, and then further north and west to Antioch. Finally, he settled in this "Babylon," which is nowhere to be found in Asia Minor. However, the ancient Christians did refer to Rome as "spiritual Babylon." Pagan Rome was the only ancient city that the New Testament refers to as "Babylon" (Revelation 17:5). Could this be what Saint Peter meant in his closing farewell to the Christians of Asia Minor? This is the most likely explanation, and one that perfectly fits with the historical record. Peter was writing from "spiritual Babylon" (Pagan Rome) to Christians he used to shepherd himself in Asia Minor. Yes, Peter was in Rome. He lived there for about 25 years (AD 42-67)[207] and

[207] Eusebius, Church History, 2, 14, 5 (AD 325)

he established his Apostolic headquarters there, bestowing his full Apostolic authority upon his successors.

Maybe Jesus did invest his authority into his Apostles, but does that mean these Apostles could really transfer that authority on to their successors?

Did the Apostles have the authority to vest others with the same authority Jesus gave to them? Let's look at what Scripture has to say about that.

After the ascension of Jesus into heaven, while the Apostles were waiting in the upper room for the Feast of Pentecost, when the Holy Spirit would come to give them power, they decided who among the one-hundred-twenty lesser disciples would replace Judas Iscariot (the fallen Apostle). They settled on Matthias and vested him with the full authority of an Apostle, completely replacing the office that Judas abandoned.[208] It was as if Jesus himself had ordained and consecrated him.

So we know the Apostles had the authority to transfer their full Apostolic authority on to others. We know the process through which this is done is by laying on hands.[209] We have historical records that plainly lay out this Apostolic succession from many of the Apostles to modern times. No such record is more clearly documented than that of St Peter (see Appendix 1).

---

[208] Acts 1:15-26

[209] 1st Timothy 4:4 & 5:22

So did the Apostles have the authority to transfer their same authority on to others? Yes! Absolutely! There is no logical or Biblical reason to doubt this. The direct successors of the Apostles are the bishops of the Catholic Church.

Why do we need Apostolic successors when we have the Bible?

It's wonderful that we have the Bible today, but let's remember that the only reason why we have the Bible (in one complete volume) is because of the work of these Apostolic successors (bishops) in the late fourth century (see Chapter 3). We also must remember that the Bible was never intended to be a catechism of systematic theology. It is a cross-section of Christian history and tradition. It's not a concise encyclopaedia of it. We also have to remember what the Bible itself says about the bishops, specifically instructing us to follow their teaching,[210] and how it calls the Church (not the Bible) "*the pillar and bulwark of the truth.*" – (1st Timothy 3:15)[211]

How can the Catholic Church really be the Church Jesus established when there are scandals and corruption?

This is a fair question. Before I answer it however, I should point out that much of the historical record concerning scandals and corruption in the Church is tainted

[210] 1st Corinthians 16:15-16; 1st Thessalonians 5:12; Hebrews 13:17
[211] Revised Standard Version Catholic Edition (RSVCE)

by those who wrote the history. In predominantly Protestant countries, like the United States for example, history is told in such a way that often favors Protestant churches over the Catholic Church.

Case in point, after years of critical review, we now know that much of the stories we were told about the inquisitions were untrue. While abuses obviously did happen, a good portion of what most people commonly think about the inquisitions was made up propaganda, put out by the English crown (which was Protestant) to defame the Catholic Church and bolster the Protestant Church of England (Anglicanism).

We know now that much of what we are told about the crusades is only half of the story. The crusades were actually a military retaliation for hundreds of years of Islamic jihad against Christianity, much in the same way the United States retaliated against al-Qaeda and the Taliban after the September 11th jihadist attacks in 2001.

We now know more about the details of the Galileo affair, in which we've learned that Galileo was tried for heresy because he attempted to reinterpret the Bible, not because he taught the heliocentric theory on the motion of planets. (That theory was also taught by many priests and professors in universities at the time who faced no such inquisition.) Galileo tried to make his theory fit with the Bible by reinterpreting the Bible apart from Church approval. He was, in effect, preaching religion and broke the Church's rule of separating science and religion. He later wrote a treatise that defended his theory but insulted the pope.[212] It was his pattern, of defying Church authority, that led to his excommunication. Officially, he was condemned as a heretic for holding (as religious truth) that the sun is the center of the entire universe. This is not true, neither in a religious sense, nor in a scientific sense.[213] Galileo was wrong on both counts. Whether or not he deserved excommunication is up for debate. (Personally, I don't think the punishment fits the crime. It was a little harsh.) Galileo was placed under house arrest for his own protection. Back then, heresy was tantamount to treason. By placing him under house arrest (in his own mansion), the state could not prosecute him.

Further investigation into the World War II records of Pope Pius XII reveal that he did more to help European Jews escape Nazi persecution than any other world leader at the time, and that no real and substantial cooperation ever existed between the Third Reich and the Holy See. Furthermore, evidence has surfaced that Hitler actually tried to have Pope Pius XII kidnapped multiple times.

Finally, a detailed investigation into the recent sexual abuse scandals in the Catholic Church has revealed that less than 5% of all clergy were involved in the sexual abuse of minors, either directly or through coverup. While this

---

[212] "The Dialogue Concerning the Two Chief World Systems" (Italian "Dialogo sopra i due massimi sistemi del mondo"), Galileo Galilei, AD 1632

[213] As proved by Monsignor Georges Lemaître in his work: "A homogeneous Universe of constant mass and growing radius accounting for the radial velocity of extragalactic nebulae," popularly referred to as the "Big Bang Theory," published in AD 1927, and eventually verified as accurate by Edwin Hubble and Albert Einstein.

statistic is painfully high, it's no higher than the statistics of similar sexual abuse cases found in all other churches and denominations. (Let us never forget the 95% of Catholic and Protestant clergy who had nothing to do with this!) It is also significantly lower, many times lower, than the type of sexual abuse of minors often found in secular (non-religious) institutions, such as public schools for example. The United States Department of Education commissioned an educational researcher, Charol Shakeshaft, to investigate the incidence of sexual abuse and coverup in America's public schools. The "Educator Sexual Misconduct" report was the first of its kind and a watershed event in this field of research. According to a 2006 National Review Online opinion column, Shakeshaft said: "*the physical sexual abuse of students in* [public] *schools is likely more than 100 times the abuse by* [Catholic] *priests.*"

So the point I'm making here is that while scandal and corruption are a real part of Church history, it's often the case that these things get exaggerated either for government propaganda reasons, or for reasons of sensationalist journalism. Scandals and corruption are real. The sensational exaggeration that surrounds them is often not real.

With that being said, are we to believe that the Church Jesus Christ established would be free of scandal and corruption? Let's take a look at ancient Israel before Christ. After all, God himself founded the ancient nation of Israel. Were they free of scandal? We know that the priests of ancient Israel once offered child sacrifices.[214] We know

[214] Jeremiah 32:32-35

that a cult of Pagan prostitutes once inhabited the Temple of the Lord in Jerusalem.[215] Did this change the identity of ancient Israel? Did Israel cease to be Israel when these things happened? No. Israel remained Israel. Nobody went out and tried to start a "another Israel" somewhere else – one that would be more "pure." Scandals and corruption were just part of the game. That's what happens when you put human beings in charge of things. In spite of this, St John the Apostle wrote that "*salvation is of the Jews.*" – (John 4:22)

Would Jesus' Church then be free of such corruption? Don't tell Jesus that, for he (knowingly of course) appointed the worst form of thief and traitor (Judas Iscariot) right into the highest levels of management within the Church at its most embryonic stage![216] Then of course, we have the cowardice of St Peter, King Jesus' own prime minister.[217] Later we see the hypocrisy of this same prime minister in Antioch.[218] All of this is typical and expected. This is what happens when human beings are put in charge of things. The Church did not cease to be the Church at this point. Nobody went out and tried to start "another Church" because the old Church was too corrupt. What was necessary in those days (as in ours) was repentance and reform, but nobody can reform an organization from the outside.

[215] 2nd Kings 23:7
[216] Mark 14:43-46
[217] Mark 14:66-72
[218] Galatians 2:11-21

Through all of this, the Catholic Church retained her identity as the new "*Israel of God.*" – (Galatians 6:16) For the Bible tells us that in spite of man's unfaithfulness, God remains faithful to the people and institutions he established.[219] Jesus himself warned us that this would happen when he told us about the parable of the weeds and the wheat,[220] and the parable of the net that collects both good fish and bad fish.[221] This is what it means to be part of an institution established by God but run by men. The occasional infidelity of the Church's leaders does not in any way nullify the Church's message of the gospel, nor does it in any way alter its identity as the Kingdom of God, the New Israel,[222] the one and only Catholic Church established by Jesus Christ.

Do Catholics really believe the pope is infallible?

Actually it's worse than that. We believe that we are infallible sometimes too. You see, sometimes we Catholics make simple arithmetic statements like: one plus one equals two. That's an infallible statement! You see it's totally accurate and "without error."

To understand we must define what is meant by the word "infallible." Contrary to popular belief, it does not mean sinless. The pope can sin, and indeed many popes

[219] Romans 3:3-4 & 2nd Timothy 2:13

[220] Matthew 13:24-30

[221] Matthew 13:47-48

[222] Galatians 6:15-16; Catechism of the Catholic Church, paragraphs 751 & 877

have sinned, starting with the first one, St Peter, when he denied our Lord three times,[223] and then later when he hypocritically denied the power of the gospel to reconcile Jewish and Gentile believers in Christ.[224] Nor does infallibility mean the pope can't make a mistake in his regular teachings or administrative acts. Yes, popes can error, even in matters of religious doctrine.[225] These errors can even be resisted by clergy and laity. Popes are not demigods. They're human.

The doctrine of papal infallibility means the pope is protected from error by the Holy Spirit, when he dogmatically defines doctrine from the Chair of Saint Peter.[226] This is when he's exercising his Biblical "binding and loosing" authority[227] as St Peter's successor. It's actually a very rare event that may only occur once or twice in a century. Many popes never use this authority at all. The last pope to use it (as of the date of this writing) was Pope Pius XII, in 1950, when he closed all arguments and doubts over the Assumption of the Blessed Virgin Mary.[228] No pope since (as of the date of this writing) has exercised this authority. That's six popes, spanning seventy years, with no infallible decrees.

---

[223] John 18:15-27

[224] Galatians 2:11-21

[225] Pope Honorius I (AD 625-638) was a confirmed heretic, and abused the papal office to spread his heresy, according to three ecumenical councils and his successor, Pope St Leo II (AD 682-683).

[226] Catechism of the Catholic Church, paragraphs 881 & 891

[227] Matthew 16:19

[228] Munificentissimus Deus, Pope Pius XII, AD 1950

When papal infallibility is used, it simply means that a particular doctrine is defined "without error" under the protection of the Holy Spirit. That's it. It means no more and no less than that. Catholics are obliged to believe the pope has settled the matter (without error) by the protection of the Holy Spirit, under the authority given to St Peter and his successors by Jesus Christ himself. If a Catholic refuses to believe it, and refuses to repent after correction, said Catholic has committed formal heresy and can be disciplined by the Church.[229]

[229] Church discipline usually consists of withholding communion from a Catholic (interdiction), and sometimes formal excommunication. Both of these disciplines can be found in Scripture (1st Corinthians 5:5, 11; Titus 3:10; Matthew 18:17; 1st Timothy 1:20; 2nd Thessalonians 3:14).

CONCLUSION

I think it's appropriate here to express my gratitude toward the Christians in the Ozarks, who have courteously (and sometimes not so courteously) posed these questions to me. While some Catholics may find these questions intimidating, I see them as a grand opportunity. I have never taken offence to them, because you see, as a former Evangelical, I too used to ask these same questions myself. Sadly, when I asked them, all those years ago, I sometimes tended to lean toward the "not so courteous" method. So in other words; I get it. I know how these good folks feel about these issues because I used to feel the exact same way.

I must confess here that I have an admiration for Evangelicals, and I'm not just saying that because I used to be one. Though I must admit that having been an Evangelical has given me insight into what it's like. This inside experience has only caused me to admire them all the more. For Evangelicals reading this book, I have no criticism. You are my Christian brethren, regardless if you accept me as yours. The Catholic Church embraces you as our Christian brethren and this is taught in the Catechism – no strings attached.[230]

It is the Evangelical fire and zeal I admire the most, as well as the Evangelical passion for learning the Scriptures. You see, Evangelicals have less resources at their disposal, from a Catholic point of view. They don't have all the sacraments, and they are especially lacking the Holy

[230] Catechism of the Catholic Church, paragraphs 818 & 1271

Eucharist. They don't have authentic holy orders backed by Apostolic succession. They don't have the wonderful Apostolic Traditions that complement Biblical teaching. They don't even have the whole Bible! Nor do they have an infallible authority structure to rely on when doctrinal disputes arise. (This, of course, has led to numerous divisions within their ranks.) Yet, in spite of this, these people have such a passion for Christ, and his written word, that it always leaves me impressed. It's a testimony for how God (the Holy Spirit) works in people's lives, regardless of their circumstances or lack of resources. Catholics could definitely learn a thing or two from these good folks. For if we Catholics would just have the same passion, zeal, and love for learning, combined with our sacraments and traditions, we could change the world! We've done it a few times in history already. There's no reason why we can't do it again.

We Catholics should be patient with Evangelicals as well. They are, whether anyone realizes it or not, the future of the Catholic Church. Evangelicals are converting to Catholicism in increasingly large numbers. While many Lapsed Catholics usually end up leaving the Church eventually, Evangelical converts tend to be the only demographic making up for the loss. So be nice to the Evangelicals. They may end up saving your parish someday, by replacing all those Lapsed Catholics who stopped going to Mass and left the Church entirely. When Evangelicals convert, they're usually "all in," and often make some of the best Catholics with the most zeal.

In case you haven't figured it out yet, this book isn't just for Evangelicals. It's for Catholics too. Because, you see, there is no reason for Catholics to ever be intimidated, or feel hostile toward, those who ask the type of questions dealt with in this book. The purpose of this book is not to be argumentative, and I would never recommend arguing with an Evangelical over religion.

Should we Catholics converse with them? Yes. Should we Catholics attempt to educate them about Catholicism? Yes! Should we Catholics argue with them? No. I wouldn't even recommend debating with them. Winning debates does not win converts. I've never seen it happen, and this is true for both sides. This book is not intended in any way to demean or belittle those who ask such challenging questions of our Catholic faith. On the contrary; were it not for such wonderful questions, there might not exist such a grand opportunity to present an explanation for our Catholic beliefs and traditions. The chance to explain not only helps others understand, but also refreshes our own understanding, and ultimately renews our faith.

That being said, I encourage an attitude of reckless cheer for Catholic readers of this book. Not only do we have nothing to be ashamed of as Catholics, but we also have nothing to be confrontational over. Ours is not only the largest Church in the world, but it's even the largest Church in the United States. One might never know that living in the Bible Belt, but it's true. Our Catholic Church is what it is, and it was here long before any of these new churches were around to question our legitimacy. Guess what? The Catholic Church will still be here long after they're gone. Over the last five-hundred years, the Catholic Church has witnessed no less than a dozen Protestant denominations come and go. In recent decades we have watched many mainline Protestant denominations crumble before our eyes, only to make way for the rise of Evangelical mega-churches. It's all very cyclic you see. These too will come and go, but the Catholic Church will remain just as she always has, because it is the only one established by Jesus Christ on Saint Peter the rock!

As you can see, we Catholics have good reasons for believing what we do, and the Catholic Church really is based on sound Biblical teaching. (Though we could just as easily say that the Bible itself is based on sound Catholic teaching.) Many Evangelicals have converted to Catholicism in recent years, and in many cases, this is for profound Biblical reasons. Such was the case with my wife and I, after intense prayer and study. Some Evangelicals have not converted, even after studying the Biblical arguments for Catholicism, but as a result of this study, they have been able to put away old fears and superstitions regarding the Catholic Church. In many ways, Catholics were the first "Bible Christians" and remain as such today. So it's fitting that we should make our home in America's Bible Belt and flourish here.

APPENDIX 1: List of Pontificates

1. St. Peter (AD 32-67)
2. St. Linus (AD 67-76)
3. St. Anacletus (Cletus) (AD 76-88)
4. St. Clement I (AD 88-97)
5. St. Evaristus (AD 97-105)
6. St. Alexander I (AD 105-115)
7. St. Sixtus I (AD 115-125) Also called Xystus I
8. St. Telesphorus (AD 125-136)
9. St. Hyginus (AD 136-140)
10. St. Pius I (AD 140-155)
11. St. Anicetus (AD 155-166)
12. St. Soter (AD 166-175)
13. St. Eleutherius (AD 175-189)
14. St. Victor I (AD 189-199)
15. St. Zephyrinus (AD 199-217)
16. St. Callistus I (AD 217-222) Callistus and the following three popes were opposed by St. Hippolytus, antipope (AD 217-236)
17. St. Urban I (AD 222-230)
18. St. Pontian (AD 230-235)
19. St. Anterus (AD 235-236)
20. St. Fabian (AD 236-250)
21. St. Cornelius (AD 251-253) Opposed by Novatian, antipope (AD 251)
22. St. Lucius I (AD 253-54)
23. St. Stephen I (AD 254-257)
24. St. Sixtus II (AD 257-258)
25. St. Dionysius (AD 260-268)
26. St. Felix I (AD 269-274)
27. St. Eutychian (AD 275-283)
28. St. Caius (AD 283-296) Also called Gaius
29. St. Marcellinus (AD 296-304)
30. St. Marcellus I (AD 308-309)
31. St. Eusebius (AD 309 or 310)
32. St. Miltiades (AD 311-314)

33. St. Sylvester I (AD 314-335)
34. St. Marcus (AD 336)
35. St. Julius I (AD 337-352)
36. Liberius (AD 352-366) Opposed by Felix II, antipope (AD 355-365)
37. St. Damasus I (AD 366-384) Opposed by Ursicinus, antipope (AD 366-367)
38. St. Siricius (AD 384-399)
39. St. Anastasius I (AD 399-401)
40. St. Innocent I (AD 401-417)
41. St. Zosimus (AD 417-418)
42. St. Boniface I (AD 418-422) Opposed by Eulalius, antipope (AD 418-419)
43. St. Celestine I (AD 422-342)
44. St. Sixtus III (AD 432-440)
45. St. Leo I (the Great) (AD 440-461)
46. St. Hilarius (AD 461-468)
47. St. Simplicius (AD 468-483)
48. St. Felix III (II) (AD 483-492)
49. St. Gelasius I (AD 492-496)
50. Anastasius II (AD 496-498)
51. St. Symmachus (AD 498-514) Opposed by Laurentius, antipope (AD 498-501)
52. St. Hormisdas (AD 514-523)
53. St. John I (AD 523-526)
54. St. Felix IV (III) (AD 526-530)
55. Boniface II (AD 530-532) Opposed by Dioscorus, antipope (AD 530)
56. John II (AD 533-535)
57. St. Agapetus I (AD 535-536) Also called Agapitus I
58. St. Silverius (AD 536-537)
59. Vigilius (AD 537-555)
60. Pelagius I (AD 556-561)
61. John III (AD 561-574)
62. Benedict I (AD 575-579)
63. Pelagius II (AD 579-590)
64. St. Gregory I (the Great) (AD 590-604)

65. Sabinian (AD 604-606)
66. Boniface III (AD 607)
67. St. Boniface IV (AD 608-615)
68. St. Deusdedit (Adeodatus I) (AD 615-618)
69. Boniface V (AD 619-625)
70. Honorius I (AD 625-638)
71. Severinus (AD 640)
72. John IV (AD 640-642)
73. Theodore I (AD 642-649)
74. St. Martin I (AD 649-655)
75. St. Eugene I (AD 655-657)
76. St. Vitalian (AD 657-672)
77. Adeodatus (II) (AD 672-676)
78. Donus (AD 676-678)
79. St. Agatho (AD 678-681)
80. St. Leo II (AD 682-683)
81. St. Benedict II (AD 684-685)
82. John V (AD 685-686)
83. Conon (AD 686-687)
84. St. Sergius I (AD 687-701) Opposed by Theodore and Paschal, antipopes (AD 687)
85. John VI (AD 701-705)
86. John VII (AD 705-707)
87. Sisinnius (AD 708)
88. Constantine (AD 708-715)
89. St. Gregory II (AD 715-731)
90. St. Gregory III (AD 731-741)
91. St. Zachary (AD 741-752) Stephen II followed Zachary, but because he died before being consecrated, modern lists omit him
92. Stephen II (III) (AD 752-757)
93. St. Paul I (AD 757-767)
94. Stephen III (IV) (AD 767-772) Opposed by Constantine II (AD 767) and Philip (AD 768), antipopes (AD 767)
95. Adrian I (AD 772-795)
96. St. Leo III (AD 795-816)
97. Stephen IV (V) (AD 816-817)

98. St. Paschal I (AD 817-824)
99. Eugene II (AD 824-827)
100. Valentine (AD 827)
101. Gregory IV (AD 827-844)
102. Sergius II (AD 844-847) Opposed by John, antipope
103. St. Leo IV (AD 847-855)
104. Benedict III (AD 855-858) Opposed by Anastasius, antipope (AD 855)
105. St. Nicholas I (the Great) (AD 858-867)
106. Adrian II (AD 867-872)
107. John VIII (AD 872-882)
108. Marinus I (AD 882-884)
109. St. Adrian III (AD 884-885)
110. Stephen V (VI) (AD 885-891)
111. Formosus (AD 891-896)
112. Boniface VI (AD 896)
113. Stephen VI (VII) (AD 896-897)
114. Romanus (AD 897)
115. Theodore II (AD 897)
116. John IX (AD 898-900)
117. Benedict IV (AD 900-903)
118. Leo V (AD 903) Opposed by Christopher, antipope (AD 903-904)
119. Sergius III (AD 904-911)
120. Anastasius III (AD 911-913)
121. Lando (AD 913-914)
122. John X (AD 914-928)
123. Leo VI (AD 928)
124. Stephen VIII (AD 929-931)
125. John XI (AD 931-935)
126. Leo VII (AD 936-939)
127. Stephen IX (AD 939-942)
128. Marinus II (AD 942-946)
129. Agapetus II (AD 946-955)
130. John XII (AD 955-963)
131. Leo VIII (AD 963-964)
132. Benedict V (AD 964)

133. John XIII (AD 965-972)
134. Benedict VI (AD 973-974)
135. Benedict VII (AD 974-983) Benedict and John XIV were opposed by Boniface VII, antipope (AD 974; 984-985)
136. John XIV (AD 983-9984)
137. John XV (AD 985-96)
138. Gregory V (AD 996-999) Opposed by John XVI, antipope (AD 997-998)
139. Sylvester II (AD 999-1003)
140. John XVII (AD 1003)
141. John XVIII (AD 1003-09)
142. Sergius IV (AD 1009-1012)
143. Benedict VIII (AD 1012-1024) Opposed by Gregory, antipope (AD 1012)
144. John XIX (AD 1024-1032)
145. Benedict IX (AD 1032-1045)* He appears on this list three separate times, see * note below
146. Sylvester III (AD 1045) Considered by some to be an antipope
147. Benedict IX (AD 1045)*
148. Gregory VI (AD 1045-1046)
149. Clement II (AD 1046-1047)
150. Benedict IX (AD 1047-1048)*
151. Damasus II (AD 1048)
152. St. Leo IX (AD 1049-1054)
153. Victor II (AD 1055-1057)
154. Stephen X (AD 1057-1058)
155. Nicholas II (AD 1058-1061) Opposed by Benedict X, antipope (AD 1058)
156. Alexander II (AD 1061-1073) Opposed by Honorius II, antipope (AD 1061-1072)
157. St. Gregory VII (AD 1073-1085) Gregory and the following three popes were opposed by Guibert ("Clement III"), antipope (AD 1080-1100)
158. Blessed Victor III (AD 1086-1087)
159. Blessed Urban II (AD 1088-1099)

160. Paschal II (AD 1099-1118) Opposed by Theodoric (AD 1100), Aleric (AD 1102) and Maginulf ("Sylvester IV", AD 1105-1111), antipopes (AD 1100)
161. Gelasius II (AD 1118-1119) Opposed by Burdin ("Gregory VIII"), antipope (AD 1118)
162. Callistus II (AD 1119-1124)
163. Honorius II (AD 1124-1130) Opposed by Celestine II, antipope (AD 1124)
164. Innocent II (AD 1130-1143) Opposed by Anacletus II (AD 1130-1138) and Gregory Conti ("Victor IV") (AD 1138), antipopes (AD 1138)
165. Celestine II (AD 1143-1144)
166. Lucius II (AD 1144-1145)
167. Blessed Eugene III (AD 1145-1153)
168. Anastasius IV (AD 1153-1154)
169. Adrian IV (AD 1154-1159)
170. Alexander III (AD 1159-1181) Opposed by Octavius ("Victor IV") (AD 1159-1164), Pascal III (AD 1165-1168), Callistus III (AD 1168-1177) and Innocent III (AD 1178-1180), antipopes
171. Lucius III (AD 1181-1185)
172. Urban III (AD 1185-1187)
173. Gregory VIII (AD 1187)
174. Clement III (AD 1187-1191)
175. Celestine III (AD 1191-1198)
176. Innocent III (AD 1198-1216)
177. Honorius III (AD 1216-1227)
178. Gregory IX (AD 1227-1241)
179. Celestine IV (AD 1241)
180. Innocent IV (AD 1243-1254)
181. Alexander IV (AD 1254-1261)
182. Urban IV (AD 1261-1264)
183. Clement IV (AD 1265-1268)
184. Blessed Gregory X (AD 1271-1276)
185. Blessed Innocent V (AD 1276)
186. Adrian V (AD 1276)
187. John XXI (AD 1276-1277)
188. Nicholas III (AD 1277-1280)

189. Martin IV (AD 1281-1285)
190. Honorius IV (AD 1285-1287)
191. Nicholas IV (AD 1288-1292)
192. St. Celestine V (AD 1294)
193. Boniface VIII (AD 1294-1303)
194. Blessed Benedict XI (AD 1303-1304)
195. Clement V (AD 1305-1314)
196. John XXII (AD 1316-1334) Opposed by Nicholas V, antipope (AD 1328-1330)
197. Benedict XII (AD 1334-1342)
198. Clement VI (AD 1342-1352)
199. Innocent VI (AD 1352-1362)
200. Blessed Urban V (AD 1362-1370)
201. Gregory XI (AD 1370-1378)
202. Urban VI (AD 1378-1389) Opposed by Robert of Geneva ("Clement VII"), antipope (AD 1378-1394)
203. Boniface IX (AD 1389-1404) Opposed by Robert of Geneva ("Clement VII") (AD 1378-1394), Pedro de Luna ("Benedict XIII") (AD 1394-1417) and Baldassare Cossa ("John XXIII") (AD 1400-1415), antipopes
204. Innocent VII (AD 1404-1406) Opposed by Pedro de Luna ("Benedict XIII") (AD 1394-1417) and Baldassare Cossa ("John XXIII") (AD 1400-1415), antipopes
205. Gregory XII (AD 1406-1415) Opposed by Pedro de Luna ("Benedict XIII") (AD 1394-1417), Baldassare Cossa ("John XXIII") (AD 1400-1415), and Pietro Philarghi ("Alexander V") (AD 1409-1410), antipopes
206. Martin V (AD 1417-1431)
207. Eugene IV (AD 1431-1447) Opposed by Amadeus of Savoy ("Felix V"), antipope (AD 1439-1449)
208. Nicholas V (AD 1447-1455)
209. Callistus III (AD 1455-1458)
210. Pius II (AD 1458-1464)
211. Paul II (AD 1464-1471)
212. Sixtus IV (AD 1471-1484)
213. Innocent VIII (AD 1484-1492)
214. Alexander VI (AD 1492-1503)

215. Pius III (AD 1503)
216. Julius II (AD 1503-1513)
217. Leo X (AD 1513-1521)
218. Adrian VI (AD 1522-1523)
219. Clement VII (AD 1523-1534)
220. Paul III (AD 1534-1549)
221. Julius III (AD 1550-1555)
222. Marcellus II (AD 1555)
223. Paul IV (AD 1555-1559)
224. Pius IV (AD 1559-1565)
225. St. Pius V (AD 1566-1572)
226. Gregory XIII (AD 1572-1585)
227. Sixtus V (AD 1585-1590)
228. Urban VII (AD 1590)
229. Gregory XIV (AD 1590-1591)
230. Innocent IX (AD 1591)
231. Clement VIII (AD 1592-1605)
232. Leo XI (AD 1605)
233. Paul V (AD 1605-1621)
234. Gregory XV (AD 1621-1623)
235. Urban VIII (AD 1623-1644)
236. Innocent X (AD 1644-1655)
237. Alexander VII (AD 1655-1667)
238. Clement IX (AD 1667-1669)
239. Clement X (AD 1670-1676)
240. Blessed Innocent XI (AD 1676-1689)
241. Alexander VIII (AD 1689-1691)
242. Innocent XII (AD 1691-1700)
243. Clement XI (AD 1700-1721)
244. Innocent XIII (AD 1721-1724)
245. Benedict XIII (AD 1724-1730)
246. Clement XII (AD 1730-1740)
247. Benedict XIV (AD 1740-1758)
248. Clement XIII (AD 1758-1769)
249. Clement XIV (AD 1769-1774)
250. Pius VI (AD 1775-1799)
251. Pius VII (AD 1800-1823)

252. Leo XII (AD 1823-1829)
253. Pius VIII (AD 1829-1830)
254. Gregory XVI (AD 1831-1846)
255. Blessed Pius IX (AD 1846-1878)
256. Leo XIII (AD 1878-1903)
257. St. Pius X (AD 1903-1914)
258. Benedict XV (AD 1914-1922)
259. Pius XI (AD 1922-1939)
260. Pius XII (AD 1939-1958)
261. St. John XXIII (AD 1958-1963)
262. Paul VI (AD 1963-1978)
263. John Paul I (AD 1978)
264. St. John Paul II (AD 1978-2005)
265. Benedict XVI (AD 2005-2013)
266. Francis (AD 2013-20??)

*Benedict IX served three times on this list. It was a scandalous situation, because he claimed the papacy in three different terms. So there have been 266 pontificates, but only 264 popes, or 263 successors of St Peter.

APPENDIX 2: The Biblical Canon

OLD TESTAMENT

1. Genesis
2. Exodus
3. Leviticus
4. Numbers
5. Deuteronomy
6. Joshua
7. Judges
8. Ruth
9. 1 Samuel
10. 2 Samuel
11. 1 Kings
12. 2 Kings
13. 1 Chronicles
14. 2 Chronicles
15. Ezra
16. Nehemiah
17. Tobit*
18. Judith*
19. Esther
20. 1 Maccabees*
21. 2 Maccabees*
22. Job
23. Psalms
24. The Proverbs
25. Ecclesiastes
26. The Song of Songs
27. Wisdom*

28. Ecclesiasticus / Sirach*
29. Isaiah
30. Jeremiah
31. Lamentations
32. Baruch*
33. Ezekiel
34. Daniel
35. Hosea
36. Joel
37. Amos
38. Obadiah
39. Jonah
40. Micah
41. Nahum
42. Habakkuk
43. Zephaniah
44. Haggai
45. Zechariah
46. Malachi

* Books removed by Martin Luther and the Protestant Reformers in the sixteenth century.

NEW TESTAMENT

1. Matthew
2. Mark
3. Luke
4. John
5. Acts of the Apostles
6. Romans
7. 1 Corinthians

8. 2 Corinthians
9. Galatians
10. Ephesians
11. Philippians
12. Colossians
13. 1 Thessalonians
14. 2 Thessalonians
15. 1 Timothy
16. 2 Timothy
17. Titus
18. Philemon
19. Hebrews
20. James
21. 1 Peter
22. 2 Peter
23. 1 John
24. 2 John
25. 3 John
26. Jude
27. Revelation

RESOURCES

1. Bible, Douay-Rheims, American Edition, AD 1899
2. Bible, Revised Standard Version – Catholic Edition, AD 1965, 1966
3. Bible, King James Version AD 1611
4. Catechism of the Catholic Church, Second Edition, Doubleday Publishing, AD 1997
5. Code of Canon Law, Vatican Online Archives, AD 1983,
6. Sacerdotalis coelibatus, Vatican Online Archives, AD 1967
7. Anglicanorum coetibus, Vatican Online Archives, AD 2009
8. Charol Shakeshaft, *Educator Sexual Misconduct Report*, U.S. Department of Education, Office of the Under Secretary, AD 2004
9. Justin Martyr, *First Apology*, AD 155
10. Ignatius of Antioch, *Epistle to the Smyrnaeans*, AD 105
11. Ignatius of Antioch, *Epistle to the Romans*, AD 105
12. Hermas, *The Shepherd*, AD 80
13. Clement of Rome, *The First Epistle of Clement*, AD 96
14. Origen, *Prayer*, AD 233
15. Origen, *Commentary on Matthew*, AD 248
16. Cyprian of Carthage, *Letters*, AD 253
17. Irenaeus, *Against Heresies*, AD 180
18. Eusebius, *Church History*, AD 325

19. Epiphanius, *Panarion*, AD 377

20. Tertullian, *Against Marcion*, AD 210

21. Tertullian, *Scorpiace*, AD 212

22. Peter of Alexandria, *The Canonical Epistle*, AD 306

23. Cyril of Jerusalem, *Catechetical Lectures*, AD 350

24. Thirty-Nine Articles of Religion, AD 1563

25. Westminster Confession of Faith AD 1647

26. Brief Statement of the Doctrinal Position of the Missouri Synod, Adopted AD 1932

27. Pope John Paul II, speech to bishops of Southern Germany, Dec. 4, 1992

28. Pope Benedict XVI, Angelus, Vatican City, February 26, 2012

29. Fr. Mario P. Romero, *Unabridged Christianity*, Queenship Publishing Company, AD 1999

30. Taylor R. Marshall, *The Crucified Rabbi*, Saint John Press, AD 2009

31. Scott Hahn, *The Lamb's Supper*, Doubleday Religion, AD 1999

32. Stephen K. Ray, *Crossing The Tiber*, Ignatius Press, AD 1997

Printed in Great Britain
by Amazon

78307623R00102